# TEXTUAL CACOPHONY

# TEXTUAL CACOPHONY

Online Video and Anonymity in Japan

**Daniel Johnson**

**CORNELL EAST ASIA SERIES**
an imprint of
**CORNELL UNIVERSITY PRESS**
**Ithaca and London**

Number 215 in the Cornell East Asia Series

Copyright © 2023 by Cornell University
All rights reserved. Except for brief quotations in a review, this book, or parts thereof, must not be reproduced in any form without permission in writing from the publisher. For information, address Cornell University Press, Sage House, 512 East State Street, Ithaca, New York 14850. Visit our website at cornellpress.cornell.edu.

First published 2023 by Cornell University Press

Library of Congress Cataloging-in-Publication Data

Names: Johnson, Daniel, 1982– author.
Title: Textual cacophony : online video and anonymity in Japan / Daniel Johnson.
Description: Ithaca : Cornell East Asia Series, an imprint of Cornell University Press, 2023. | Series: Cornell East Asia series ; number 215 | Includes bibliographical references and index. | Summary: "Textual Cacophony discusses online media in Japan, with a focus on how anonymity and asynchronous media interfaces impact the aesthetic and cultural practices of users of Niconico, 2channel, and related social media platforms"— Provided by publisher.
Identifiers: LCCN 2022059794 (print) | LCCN 2022059795 (ebook) | ISBN 9781501772252 (hardcover) | ISBN 9781501772269 (paperback) | ISBN 9781501772276 (epub) | ISBN 9781501772283 (pdf)
Subjects: LCSH: Digital media—Social aspects—Japan. | Social media and society—Japan. | Social media—Japan. | Online social networks—Japan. | Internet videos—Japan. | Online identities—Japan.
Classification: LCC HM742 .J534 2023 (print) | LCC HM742 (ebook) | DDC 302.23/10952—dc23/eng/20230206
LC record available at https://lccn.loc.gov/2022059794
LC ebook record available at https://lccn.loc.gov/2022059795

# Contents

Illustrations — vii
Acknowledgment — ix
Note on Romanization — xi

Introduction: Lost in the Crowd — 1
1. Animated Writing — 24
2. Characters of Language — 42
3. Repertoire and Accumulation — 64
4. Collecting, Copying, and Copyright — 84
5. Scripted Laughter — 101
Postscript: Out of Time — 129

Notes — 139
Works Cited — 149
Index — 157

# Illustrations

**0.1.** UStream coverage of anti-Korean protesters at Fuji TV's Odaiba campus — 3

**0.2.** Niconico comment feed from Team Neko's I Can't Beat Airman — 11

**0.3.** *Telop* subtitle from Japanese variety television — 13

**1.1.** Google's Japanese input method editor — 38

**2.1.** Comment art depicting Airman, from Mega Man 2 — 48

**2.2.** Comment art tracing a dancer's movements on Niconico — 49

**2.3.** Song lyrics rendered as moving text — 50

**2.4.** Comment art (two examples) — 55

**3.1.** "Mishearing" for comedic effect on Niconico — 73

**3.2.** Comment art counting times an anime character has been struck — 74

**3.3.** Repeated joke of "mishearing" in Blood Clan video from Niconico — 81

**4.1.** Niconico-style comments simulated on TV *Yonpara: Future Battle* — 97

**5.1.** Comments making fun of a playthrough of Mario 64 — 116

**5.2.** Comments joking about a playthrough of Super Mario Bros 3 — 117

**5.3.** Pixel game art in P-P's playthrough of Super Mario Bros 3 — 118

**5.4.** Comment feed from video playthrough of Dead Space — 119

# Acknowledgment

Sections of chapter 1 and chapter 2 previously appeared in "Polyphonic/Pseudo-synchronic: Animated Writing in the Comment Feed of Nicovideo," *Japanese Studies* 33, no. 3: 297–313. Those ideas are presented here with the permission of the publisher.

# A Note on Japanese Names, Romanization, and Translation

Names appear in Japanese order, with family name first and personal name second. In the text, English translations sometimes appear, followed by romanized transliterations of the Japanese in parentheses. In the "Works Cited" list, English translations are given in brackets for the titles of Japanese-language works cited, following romanized transliterations of the Japanese. Macrons are used to indicate long vowels for most words transliterated from Japanese, with the exception being words and place names that frequently appear in English (such as Tokyo). Some words that appear in katakana are also provided with a double vowel rather than a macron to preserve a sense of distinction from other scripts.

# TEXTUAL CACOPHONY

# INTRODUCTION
Lost in the Crowd

On July 23, 2011, the actor Takaoka Sousuke posted a series of comments to his Twitter account criticizing Fuji TV, one of the major commercial television networks in Tokyo. These messages included complaints about the channel's airing of South Korean–made television dramas and featuring South Korean popular music acts on their variety shows. His tirade began, "Even though they've been good to me in the past, I seriously don't watch 8 [Fuji TV] anymore. It's like they've become a Korean TV station." He elaborated on his position in subsequent tweets, writing "I feel like 'what country is this?!' . . . It makes me sick, like brainwashing" and "This is Japan, right? I want to see them do Japanese shows. And have Japanese songs." Anti-Korean discourse has had a significant presence in Japanese-language internet culture for many years, but Takaoka's outburst against Fuji Television and its perceived alliance with South Korean media was unusual in that these were statements being made by a public figure involved in the entertainment industry.

Many users of social media were quick to criticize Takaoka's comments for their nationalistic tone. Others simply enjoyed the media content from South Korea and didn't see what the big deal was. However, a significant minority of users rallied behind these expressions of frustration with the perceived embrace of Korean popular culture by Japanese media. Takaoka's remarks were echoed in online media such as blogs, the video-sharing site Niconico, and the web forum 2channel, all of which have served as incubation chambers for right-wing (*uyoku*) discourses in Japanese-language internet media.[1] It wasn't long before the situation grew from Takaoka's initial declarations posted to Twitter and spun into a larger discourse of anti-Korean activism and general resentment toward mainstream mass media in Japan.[2] Within days, anti-Korean users of social media began piggy-backing on this surge of online activity around the topic, using Twitter alongside 2channel and Niconico to organize protests outside of Fuji Television's headquarters in Odaiba, Tokyo.

Anti-Korea protesters appeared on the grounds of Fuji Television's campus on August 7, 2011. Many attendees carried signs criticizing the network for broadcasting Korean-made dramas, for the appearance of Korean performers on Fuji's variety shows, and due to a general suspicion of the forging of the popularity of South Korean media in Japan by the network for its own gain.[3] Reporters from sites such as UStream and Niconico were also present at the event to provide online coverage, bringing cameras to film the protesters and stream live feeds of the event for audiences at home (see fig. 0.1). Many viewers watched on personal computers, but the widespread availability of internet-ready mobile phones also allowed virtual attendance in the protest. Users from across Japan and even overseas chimed in with messages posted to social media services such as Twitter. Over ten thousand online viewers checked in over the course of the day through a variety of different web services. Live attendance was estimated at around six hundred.

However, while the protest was well attended, peacefully orchestrated, and gained a surprisingly large following online, it also coincided with the famous United States of Odaiba (*Odaiba gashukoku*) event that Fuji Television holds every summer. This event was created to celebrate the network's brand identity and promote its broadcast lineup and stable of performers. Guest appearances by celebrities, live concerts, and special activities for fans to participate in were some of the main attractions. An unexpected consequence of this timing was that the columns of marching protesters moving throughout the campus of the network found themselves sharing the same space with crowds of tourists and fans who were there to enjoy the festivities. Audiences watching on UStream and Niconico quickly picked up on this dynamic, noting the way that the protesters were becoming difficult to distinguish from the regular visitors who were attending the Odaiba campus that day. This led audiences who were watching online to turn on their would-be allies and begin mocking the protesters, who, in the eyes of these viewers, appeared ridiculous as they were caught between roving bands of enthusiastic TV fans and tourists. The sense of urgency and outrage that initially propelled the protest against Fuji TV (as well as the support that those sentiments had found online) thus quickly found itself being deflated by ridicule. Coverage of the event and plans for further protests continued into the following weeks, but, for at least part of the online audience, the operation had quickly lost its initial significance and became a big joke.

**FIGURE 0.1.** Footage from UStream's coverage of anti-Korean protesters at Fuji TV's Odaiba campus on August 7, 2011. One user (second from the top in the right-hand chat window) ironically comments "what an amazing parade!" (*sugoi sanpo da!*).

## Stuck in the Middle with Who?

The episode described above captures some of the tendencies I find most striking about online media culture in Japan. These include the ambivalent relationship between internet culture and television, the emphasis on irony and the self-presentation of disengagement in how users interact with one another, and the fissures of time between asynchronous, online discourse and real time, offline events. This incident is also useful for introducing the comparatively unexamined topic of internet anonymity alongside more familiar notions of offline, real-world identities and ideologies, such as nationality and nationalism. With those things in mind, there is a lot to unpack from even this single example and what it represents of contemporary Japan and online media cultures.

English-language research on internet media in Japan frequently casts its attention on the relationship between the nation and online culture to understand the behaviors and ideologies of Japanese media users, with topics such as aggressive, reactionary politics (similar to those described above) forming a significant part of how online communities have been studied by scholars in fields such as anthropology and media studies. This approach can be found in studies of xenophobia (Yamaguchi 2013) and right-wing political activism in Japanese media (Hall 2021). Interest in how language is used in online platforms has provided another pillar in the study in Japanese internet culture, with many scholars writing on topics related to different forms of expression related to gender, sexuality, and code-switching (Robertson 2022).

This book will elaborate on these trajectories but also shift the frame of analysis to consider language not in terms of direct expressions of individual identity or denotational meaning but rather as a kind of shared energy or affect that users are able to participate in through opaque forms of writing in an anonymous sphere of communication. In that sense, the goal in understanding the relationship between language and identity for this project will not be focused on individual expressions of said forms but rather in how those are adopted by an aggregate audience in a performative manner—a kind of virtual playing of a character or role that is shared across a body of users. This stylization of identity in turn provides a way of generating an alternative mode of rapport and belonging between users that appears to promise (but not necessarily fulfill) a resolution to the social and cultural gaps produced by the degradation of traditional social institutions in contemporary Japan.

This approach doesn't mean doing away with the nation as a category for understanding online culture in Japan. Rather, I reconsider the relationship between actual-world and online social formations and identities as not exhaustive of one another. I see this relationship as porous and flexible, with things like laughter and play becoming routines for restaging political sentiment in online spaces without needing to directly reproduce it cohesively. The opacity of anonymous communication and its reliance on deviant script and asynchronous temporalities renders online media and identities as ironic, bracketed by new forms of meaning that add layers of mediation and confusion in the process. This bracketing of meaning by routines of play, laughter, and opacity is the conceptual space this study will inhabit in considering how the complicated relationship of online culture to the actual world can be understood. It is also a way of attending to online media culture on something closer to its own terms.

Returning to the scene of Odaiba and the Fuji TV protests of 2011 can help clarify some of these distinctions about identity and media in contemporary Japan. Looking at the behavior of the online crowds that watched the in-person demonstrators from behind their screens, we can observe a simultaneous divergence from and reproduction of actual-world understandings of personal identity. Online cultures of anonymity have frequently been linked to a tendency toward a certain kind of elitism in which new categories of identification appear in a way that simultaneously disavow and replicate actual-world identities concerning race, gender, and class. Specific designations of identity might change or become less visible due to the anonymity afforded to individuals, but the overall structure of privilege and difference often remains in some way through discursive routines. The behavior of the online spectators laughing at the Fuji

Television protest gestures toward one version of this notion, with this particular example also being tempered by a nationalistic, anti-Korean sensibility, a local instance of the type of aggression and suspicion directed toward members of minority communities that can be found in online discourse around the world.[4]

From a more abstract perspective, the form of elitism being demonstrated here might also be one characterized as a politics of being "apart from." We can understand this notion of distance in that the online users are able to watch footage from the site of the protest while not actually being present in that space. But this sense of being "apart from" also appears through the self-presentation of disengagement, of being able to mock the protesters without being materially involved in those events. This sense of being unmarked by one's individual identity—or even being untroubled by questions of identity in general—also plays a significant part in the politics of anonymity. This might also be coupled with the feeling of enjoying a lack of commitment to any specific idea or politics. Just as one's identity disappears into the aggregate mass, so does one's responsibility to a given politics or action. The cultural and aesthetic practices of online anonymity invite such a mode of ambivalent (dis)identification, but this sensibility also aligns with larger concerns in late capitalism, such as the frustration of identity through thwarted political agency, and the visual chaos and disorientation of contemporary screen culture.[5]

That tendency toward political disengagement and disavowing identity plays a significant part in online culture. It is a kind of self-presentation that avoids the anchor of identification but still enjoys the perspective of actual-world experience, overlapping with the fantasy of personal autonomy associated with neoliberalism but also stemming from the social and economic precarity that has arisen for so many people in contemporary Japan, in which the once heralded model of lifelong employment has given way to short-term contracts and underemployment.[6] And while many of these routines of self-presentation can be found in different parts of the world, this form of anonymous self-presentation also provides a historical anchor to the political and cultural life of post-bubble Japan coinciding with more commonly recognized issues such as social reclusiveness among younger generations (*hikikomori*), the rise of suicide due to pressures at school (often associated with bullying), and physical and mental exhaustion at work.[7] These all speak to the widespread social atomization found in post-bubble Japan and point toward some of the ways that withdrawal from mainstream society has become not only more common but also more attractive to many individuals, as the previous model of "group living" (*shudan seikatsu*) and collective goals in education and the workforce has waned (Slater 2010). As Anne Allison has noted, these patterns of withdrawal often coincide with an "inability to find comfort in society as it exists" due to the breakdown of familiar institutions of family, work, and schooling (Allision 2013, 74). The cultural play of anonymity can feel as if it offers a liberating alternative or outlet within this context, promising a form of mobility in online identity, freedom of expression, and political involvement that one can't necessarily enjoy in actual world situations.

That sense of disavowal cannot, however, explain everything that online anonymity offers. Intersecting notions of gag-like (*neta-teki*) communication that rely on mass repetition (such as memes) and an aesthetics of copied and pasted text and images together represent another way individual instances of communication and authorship begin to regress through anonymous writing. Both speak to the desire for a different form of social experience but also reflect an aesthetic of distraction from the messiness of actual world identities and suggest an alternative horizon of cultural belonging. More directly, this confluence of humor and repetition transforms acts of reading and writing into a kind of play, returning user attention and experience to the surface of the screen, where text and images move before our eyes. And if online media offers new relief from the oppressiveness of everyday life in post-bubble Japan, it might well be that potential (however illusionary) for a different kind of belonging and social existence, one that promises to provide new types of connections and feelings of coming together even as conventional social bonds are increasingly made abstract (if not isolated) and communication displaced from face-to-face interactions to highly mediated proxies.

To again return to the episode at Fuji TV, what I find most compelling about this case of deflated nationalism is the rapid transformation of online support for the political urgency of the protest into seemingly uncommitted forms of laughter and mockery. The tendency to treat everything as a big joke and to laugh ironically from the vantage point granted by anonymity is something we can find across a variety of internet media, from "in jokes" on 2channel that lampoon and troll everyone to the performance of failure in online video and streaming media and the tendency of Niconico users to poke fun—at the singers, dancers, and other amateur performers—via messages posted to the comment feed.[8] While the obvious prejudice and nationalism of Takaoka's rants on Twitter and the protests that followed are perhaps the most immediately salient characteristic of this series of events (and place it most clearly in an actual-world political space), the ambivalent reaction of the audiences watching online is instructive about the behaviors and attitudes of online media users.

## Interstitial Dimensions

Many of the behaviors and routines described above have been able to take shape and thrive due to the climate of anonymity on sites such as Niconico and

2channel. Anonymity in online media is a concept that appears straightforward at first. It is part of everyday life for many users of the internet but also challenges our understanding of issues related to data collection, media surveillance, and even how political campaigns are financed. There are, however, many distinct versions of this concept that we can observe across different sites. Identifying some of these particulars is important before moving on to the describing the scope of this book in greater detail.

Social media services such as Twitter allow the use of persistent pseudonyms or handles for users to go by. Many users go by their real names, but the presence of pseudonyms allows for a degree of anonymity that still attaches communication to a single, identifiable account that has all its postings attributed in the same way. This type of media can be characterized as pseudo-anonymous due to its engagement with both a register of masquerade that conceals the name and actual-world identity of the user behind that account but also anchors those communications to a single user account, allowing other users to follow messages, talkback posts, and retweets back to the same account. Twitter users can become famous for their content but this is often as a type of character.[9] There is also usually a greater sense of permanence with these types of platforms, which produce archives of information bound to a single account, linked to others through shared messages, correspondence, and platform-specific actions.

An important distinction between this type of pseudo-anonymity and unattributed forms of anonymity is the presence of social prestige that users can obtain and foster through developing an online personality that can be recognized across postings and usage. This is the popular model on many English language message boards such as reddit, where users can accumulate a kind of persona or identity even while remaining largely anonymous in their actual day-to-day existences. Conversely, Japanese language media such as the web forum 2channel and the video-sharing site Niconico allow for users to post messages without permanent attribution. Niconico does employ permanent user accounts that have discrete names and are tied to email accounts, but comments made to videos are not able to be traced back to an individual user or the account behind the post. This allows messages to be posted without attribution or a legible sense of authorship. While the site was still active, 2channel featured no permanent form of attribution for users. Messages posted to a thread were assigned a temporary identification number that was good for that thread but did not attach to a user's account when posting in other threads. This too relieved users of the need for even pseudo-anonymous forms of representation. Questions of prestige or individual recognition are thus less relevant, as the cultural identity of the site and its aggregate user base comes to define how users communicate with one another and engage with what they interpret to be the role of a user of that particular site.

Unattributed writing of this style has become one of the primary modes of enabling the fantasy of unmarked selfhood. This is one of the fundamental elements that allows for online anonymity and the ability to appear as a voiceless nobody in a constellation of similarly unidentified users. It can create a tension between outrageous and colorful forms of writing as image-making (such as copypasta ASCII art) but also disengages from questions of authorship or cultural capital in writing. This can be observed in any number of cases, whether it be the cacophonous style of *danmaku* commenting on a video being shown on Niconico, in which user comments rush over a video screen and even block out the video image, or an image macro meme originating on the picture board Futaba Channel. That mode of textual reproduction is part of the aesthetics of cacophonous media in Japan and the shift toward aggregate modes of representation in which the polyphonic, chattering mass of indistinct voices precludes the voice of the individual. Those aesthetics instead favor opacity as both a mode of engagement and as a mode of identification.

One cultural form that emerges from this anonymity entails a dynamic of invisibility and spectacle. I refer to styles of writing that, in their unattributed nature, render the author as invisible or indistinguishable but at the same time engage with playful and even aesthetically aggressive forms of text production. This includes the use of deliberate mistypes in Japanese and the mixing of different styles of orthography, using full-width and half-width input commands. This dynamic is one of the key aspects of Japanese-language online media.

These modes of representation render writing from something one individual does to something that happens between users in an aggregate cultural form. The patterns of energetic, extra-denotational writing and copypasta art that endlessly reproduce the same content even as they are being deleted, archived, or otherwise made invisible should similarly be understood as part of this dynamic of anonymity, asynchronicity, opacity, and spectacle. Some of the previously described types of internet discourse suggest also the aesthetic element of anonymous conduct in written Japanese, which accentuates the need to approach anonymity not just as an absence of names or attribution but also as a mode of discourse production that has its own logics of representation not bound to the individual. The aesthetics of anonymity will therefore also be an important component of this book's investigation and more broadly serve as a guide for thinking about how to read this type of linguistic practice.

Indeed, the prevalence of practices such as copy pasted writing and seemingly endless circulation of image macros and memes gesture toward some of the ways individual authorship might be exchanged for a general sense of circulation through an aggregate form of membership or community.[10] Individual authorship becomes less important, and reading and recognition of cultural cues assume the work of identification. As Tom Boellstorff has noted, text-based communication is the material foundation for online anonymity.[11] The consumption of visual information provides a locus for alternative modes of identification. This kind of text production can therefore be thought of as an expression of its own virtual materiality in addition to being a mode of representation for its users. In other words, the ways that users produce writing via online communications media, such as by copying and pasting materials from other sources or by adding text to images, is as significant as what they write.

Returning once more to the opening anecdote about Takaoka Sousuke and Fuji TV, we can observe how online anonymity is also deeply connected to the cultural logic of aggregate social forms. We have images of a mass of protesters that seemingly vanish into a larger group of tourists, staff, and other attendees at Odaiba's campus. This itself calls forth an idea of the individual disappearing into an anonymous crowd, each losing any trace of his or her own distinct identity in the rolling tide of a swarm of nonindividuals. But the audience watching online is also a kind of crowd that resists individual identity in favor of an orientation toward opacity and ambiguity. The audience laughs together at the situation of the protesters, communicating through pseudo-anonymous messages on UStream and Twitter or unattributed comments on Niconico in a way that renders the sense of chatter between users as a general discourse that allows individual users to figuratively disappear into the online crowd. This is not to say that the users of online media communicate with a single, monolithic voice, but, rather, they do so through an aggregate dynamic that allows for them to speak *through* the notion of the online crowd. Individual messages become lost in the wave of content, producing dis-identification of the individual contribution. In other words, this type of anonymity allows them to communicate as part of the site's cultural form without representing themselves as discrete, individual users. It enables a certain masquerade of identity and social responsibility that intersects with issues of unmarked privilege and resentment toward identity. Such a routine is still performed in a way that allows them to maintain their actual-world identities, reproducing sentiments of nationalism, racism, and a sense of superiority over those who do not enjoy the same privileged mode of representation.

## Visual Cacophony

As with anonymity, asynchronicity can similarly appear in a variety of ways in online media. The "pseudo-synchronicity" of sites such as Niconico (as well as

Chinese-language derivatives such as Bilibili and AcFun) provides a sense of "live" or continuous activity between users despite the actual gaps in time and experience between each instance of use.[12] This is accomplished through the projection of user comments onto a video image, with the comments timed to appear during the point in the video's playing at which they were input. The result is that messages appear as if they were addressing the content of the video in real time—or at least with a sense of coordination that implies synchronicity. We can also observe much more straightforward examples, such as the "selective synchronicity" of Twitter in which response to messages appears to produce the feeling of a conversation between users even though each message has been sent independently of the previous. Read from the perspective of the present, they appear to be a linear, continuous stream of replies and responses that amount to a conversation. The actual timing of their input and more complicated sense of linearity (or nonlinearity) are easily overlooked through this presentation of "as if" synchronicity.

The technologically produced feeling of liveness and of watching alongside other spectators suggested by the media interface on sites such as Niconico is something that is achieved despite the actual-world atomization of each user's viewing experiences. That combination of inviting a feeling of "as if" simultaneity that still maintains communicative and temporal distance between users forms an important part of how this type of online media acts to recover some sense of belonging for its audience. Another aesthetic dimension to this style of interface is the sheer volume of text that can appear over the image. Waves of comments can threaten to obscure what the video originally shows, create new forms of image-making, or otherwise draw our attention in multiple directions and toward different registers of visual content. An image from a video made for the parody song "Can't Beat Airman" demonstrates this through the use of different colors of text repeating the same expression, accompanied by nonlinguistic symbols that provide an audio spectrum visualization for the music (see fig. 0.2). This tidal wave of comments has come to be known as "barrage," or *danmaku*, a term that Xiqing Zheng traces to how fans discussed Touhou Project "bullet hell" shooter games and visual effects in 1980s television animation in Japan.[13]

Another point of comparison is the colorful, animated text and subtitles of Japanese variety television, which will often play with its relationship with the speech of onscreen performers. The resultant confusion of sound and image can be found in an even more pronounced manner in the waves of moving comments on Niconico, which do not produce literal sounds but do result in something like sonic volume and cacophony. This adds a sensory dimension to electronic text despite its bare presentation. We can observe this feeling of cacophony in the sheer number of comments that might appear in a given video

**FIGURE 0.2.** Waves of comments play over an animated video for Niconico's I Can't Beat Airman, with the lyric "no matter how many times I try" (*nan kai yatte mo*) repeated in different colors of text. The rush of comments is timed to match the singing of the lyrics.

feed or thread and also the speed with which they appear, the way they seem to contribute to an acceleration of energy, and how the language being used often replicates speech as written text. What we have appears as a mass of people talking over one another, coming across as not as a conversation but as a din or voices competing for attention and producing barely legible dialogues. As such, what we find in these media is a transformation of text into a noisy clamor that is a mix of distraction and nonsense alongside individual utterances.

The noisy, aesthetic overlap between sound and script, combined with the anonymous mode of communication and asynchronous design, produces an energy in which communication is always mediated and deferred. It is also rendered as playful and expressive in a way that allows the social atomization of online communication to somehow feel more personal, with things like style in communication standing in for other forms of personal identification. As this book will argue, the prioritization of things like style and repetition of familiar expressions in this type of media becomes central to how individual users navigate their own experience with that of the online, anonymous aggregate. This in turn becomes part of the logic through which actual-world matters of social and cultural identity are reframed through the routines of online culture and its ambivalent relationship with the actual world.

Cacophony in online text performs a deliberate confusion of different aesthetic registers and of online and offline values of identification. This tension isn't explicitly resolved via the routines of playful writing and reading that users of Niconico and 2channel engage in. But the slippery noise – the "textual cacophony" – of that ambivalence is made to generate a kind of meaning and even a feeling of community by rendering physical distance into social proximity and anonymous aggregates into casual association.

Visually cacophonous media featuring waves of electronic text projected over a video image forms a significant part of contemporary media culture in East Asia. This regional style of online video stands in contrast to the more global and commercial model suggested on YouTube, Vimeo, and Dailymotion, platforms that separate user comments from video content.[14] That use of electronic text reprioritizes the relationship between the video image and user responses, destabilizing linear understanding of how media production and authorship function (and, more abstractly, even where those categories begin and end). User attention is similar reordered, as the comments and video images compete with one another to command our gaze. As aesthetics in digital culture and non-Western instances of media convergence, this style of text-laden video is a compelling object of study for scholars of contemporary media. From a more specific perspective, more aligned with the aims of this book, such media also provide a unique meeting point for thinking about how technological mediated notions of "liveness" alter our social experiences in network culture and how anonymous communication and cultural production thrive in media interfaces that rely on unattributed electronic text. Such interfaces facilitate the transformation of text into new forms of visual spectacle and image production. They are expressive media forms, ones that suggest a very different register of representation and identification than familiar Western platforms such as YouTube.

We should also ask why this style of text-driven media emerged in Japan, and why at this particular point in time. These questions can help locate the rise of media forms such as Niconico within a special cultural and media industry context. Niconico appeared hot on the heels of YouTube in late 2006 and initially served as something of an extension of the net culture that had already been growing out of 2chan and blogs since the late 1990s and early 2000s. Many of the popular memes, forms of language used, and practices of anonymity that fueled Niconico in its early days were brought over from 2channel. We can therefore approach this type of online video as a response to other parts of internet culture during this period. However, the combination of text and image is also something we can find in other forms of screen-based media in and around Japan.

Television, mobile phones and electronic billboard advertisements in Japan all rely on a barrage of visual information that mix text and image. The information clutter of contemporary media production in East Asia frequently follows the visual logic of advertising: aggressive attention-seeking and bombardment with all manner of messages and images, often repurposed from other media forms.[15] More specifically, the use of colorful subtitles and captions to transcribe dialogue and add sarcastic commentary has been a staple of Japanese variety television since the early 1990s (Sakamoto 1999). For example, the 2010s comedy variety program *Banana Cram School* (Tokai TV) uses a TV *telop* effect to clarify a joking reference to a popular television commercial featuring Hayashi Osamu, transforming the actor into a cartoon figure as the members of the cast repeat his catchphrase "Why not now?" (fig. 0.3). These types of titles provide audiovisual redundancy to the banter between performers but also exaggerate the cluttered nature of the screen and expand the visual assault on the viewer. Similar types of comedy and talk programs in Taiwan and South Korea have adopted their graphical display systems to provide the same sort of clarification and opacity in the interplay between speech, text, and image. And as I shall describe in chapter 4, this appropriation of televisual text in online media isn't just a matter of aesthetic similarity between media forms but rather part of a circulation of media performance routines across screen types and audiences.

**FIGURE 0.3.** An example of a *telop* subtitle from *Banana Cram School* (*Banana jyuku*), a variety show that ran on Tokai Television from 2012 to 2014. The subtitle and added image supplement the line said by the three performers *(Ima desho*, or "Do it now!") and refer to the source of the catchphrase, a Toyota commercial featuring Hayashi Osamu.

## The Potential to Be Overlooked

Focused on Japan and East Asia more broadly as places with specific media platforms and cultures that shape one another, this book will examine how language figures into the visual culture of online media. Written Japanese presents many opportunities for developing alternative modes of representation in anonymous communication. As will be discussed in chapters 1 and 2, the deliberate and creative use of mistyping that engages with orthographic and figural play allows for routines expressing deindividualized membership and cultural knowledge in online communities. In Japanese this can be accomplished by choosing a nonstandard character that has the same phonetic reading as the standard character for a word or phrase, which can then be deciphered by the knowing reader. Chapter 3 will continue this discussion in relation to practices such as copypasta writing and aggregate content curation, practices that signal not just the persistence of digital labor in online communities but also how individual authorship is deemphasized in favor of an aesthetics of accumulation and distributed agency. These are all forms of writing that draw on the unique properties of computer-based writing forms to engage with aesthetic and cultural modes of expression, forms we can associate with both online anonymity and emerging routines of spectacle. As mentioned previously, this intersection of anonymity and spectacle also offers an opportunity to pursue questions of self-presentation in contemporary media culture as well as more general concerns related to the frustration of individual identity under late capitalism.

Japanese-language internet media provide many examples for this dynamic. Users on sites such as the bulletin board 2channel and the video-sharing site Niconico frequently use the personal pronoun *ore* to refer to themselves. There are over a dozen personal pronouns in Japanese, with each expressing varying nuances of formality and gender marked identity. *Ore* is an informal, if not slightly rough, word for "me," but it is also typically encoded as masculine. Using this word over alternatives such as *watashi* (formal and gender-neutral) or *boku* (masculine and slightly boyish) therefore projects a certain kind of self-presentation, one that draws on and engages with the way that term is used in everyday life and, perhaps more significantly, in film and television. Many users will similarly refer to other users of the site as *omae* or *omaera*, meaning "you" or "you guys," respectively. These terms also carry an informal and masculine nuance, equivalent in tone to the laddish qualities of *ore*. That being said, the use of gender-marked language does not always index a user of that particular gender or identity, so what emerges from these patterns of expression should also be attended to.

To begin, it should go without saying that not everyone on these sites uses this type of language. There is a wealth of discrete cultures and cohorts that exist on each site, many of which overlap. Reading through page after page of threads on 2channel or through the comment feed of video after video on Niconico, one can't help but notice the abundant use of such language and how it appears to be almost naturalized among the user base. But even among the significant number of users who do employ this language, surely not all are male or masculine, and even among the users who use *ore* and *omaera*, not all of them would speak this way in actual-world, everyday exchanges. There is, then, a gap between online and actual-world presentations of identity. One of the most striking qualities of this dynamic—this intersection of unattributed, anonymous writing with gendered language—is that it simultaneously universalizes that language while also disavowing its gender-marked qualities. In other words, as long as "everyone" uses language such as *ore* to refer to themselves, that particular type of gendered language becomes a marker of belonging among the communities on 2channel and Niconico. It presents its user base with a flattening of traditional social hierarchies, a quality that Monica Heller has connected with the rhetorical strategies of neoliberalism (Heller 2010, 106). The gendered element of *ore* is, however, also preserved even as it is made opaque. Everyone is marked as if a general, masculine user, while that gendered quality is also rendered invisible or able to be overlooked. This is one of the mundane areas in which we can perceive this dynamic between anonymous writing and something like spectacle. Spectacle can thus be understood not only as something that draws attention to itself (or its author) but also as disavowing the materials through which it garners attention. In order to better understand this tension, we can turn to the concept of being overlooked.

In writing on the relationship between software, computational writing, and ideology, Alex Galloway has noted that programming language wants to be "overlooked."[16] This is part of an effort to connect language and software to the visual (and therefore the ideological) but also to identify how the process of making something visible or explicit via expression is counterbalanced by an impulse to make the syntax of that same means of expression opaque (Galloway, 321). Computer code and computational writing are forms of textual expression and discursive production very different from the kinds of social media writing (*kakikomi*) that will discussed throughout this book, but I still wish to borrow Galloway's notion of being overlooked and its relation to computer-based text that bears no trace of individual authorship. Galloway's point about how software interfaces represent control and protocol functions has some resonance with how I will approach the issue of representation in unattributed forms of writing. The tangible machine is rendered invisible in favor of the software interface, and similarly the material body of the writing user is rendered opaque through ideologically charged language.[17] Being overlooked is part of a routine of obfuscation that hides actual-world connections and material identities.

Referring once more to words such as *ore* and *omaera* being so prevalent in anonymous Japanese-language internet communication, this notion of being overlooked or even of wanting to be overlooked can prove fruitful in analyzing how anonymous writing engages in different registers of self-presentation, spectacle, and even ideological (re)production. Within the context of online anonymity, this perhaps demonstrates a desire to be overlooked as an individual user and recognized only as part of the aggregate social form of a site's culture. But it also speaks to the ambivalent, interstitial logic of online network culture, which simultaneously disavows actual-world experience and structures of meaning while relying on those same materials in offering something that can appear new and as an alternative to existing modes of being.

There are, of course, many other kinds of online text production that we might consider as registering a desire to be overlooked or a quality of being overlooked. In addition to language that bears a strong relationship to actual-world identities (such as those marked by gender, race, or class), linguistic expression that foregrounds the very problem of reading and comprehending text provides an additional perspective to use in approaching this issue. The aforementioned barrage-style commenting provides another example for considering this dynamic. The barrage of user-generated messages in the comment feed of Niconico attracts our attention, but the speed at which they move and sheer volume of text makes them practically unreadable. One wave of messages swarms over and obscures those that came before them, giving a visual impression of activity and motion more than legible conversation or intelligible communication. This is language and writing that, while clearly spectacular, also tends toward being overlooked in terms of being able to locate authorship or even linguistic meaning. There is neither center to ground the activity on the video screen nor a voice to attach it to.

This is a very different way of approaching online anonymity than what we find in popular media coverage of online media, which tends to stress the secrecy and perceived danger of who or what lurks behind the other side of the screen in online social spaces, of how hidden identities allow for abusive behavior such as harassment campaigns. However, this dynamic of opacity and spectacle is also an important part of many users' everyday experiences with online media and speaks to another element of how anonymity can be thought of as containing its own cultural practices. Some of the above-described cultures of writing demonstrate this idea through their mobilization of figural aesthetics that, while perhaps drawing attention to the text itself, are also part of an environment of unattributed writing in which authorship is deprioritized. The spectacle allows for displacement of the register of representation away from the individual and toward the network of belonging. This dynamic can extend to other practices as well. Shunsuke Nozawa has described certain forms and practices of anonymity in Japan as engaging with "counter spectacularity."[18] This includes everyday, mundane actions such as wearing a mask over one's face while riding a train, which before the COVID 19 pandemic was sometimes perceived as having more to do with reducing one's "to-be-looked-at-ness" than for guarding against the spread of contagion.[19] These routines of counter spectacle are another form of being overlooked, of becoming invisible, and of fitting into a social and political world of economic vulnerability and precarious social possibilities. But they also connect to anonymity in that they frequently prioritize an aggregate dynamic over one representing the individual. Becoming lost in a crowd (as was described in the anecdote about the protest outside of Fuji TV's campus) is one form of being overlooked, of becoming counter-spectacular.

Asynchronous media offers another dimension to this dynamic. By allowing for discrete instances of use to appear as if part of the same moment or even conversation, asynchronicity in media such as message boards, Twitter, and the comment feed on Niconico helps us to overlook the separation in experience between users and emphasize the feeling of continuity. Actions or messages that may have occurred days, weeks, and even years ago can appear to part of a single, unbroken sequence of events that contribute to the same aggregation of user activity or feeling of togetherness. We can still observe each piece and how it might exist on its own, but the presentation of a whole vis-à-vis asynchronicity helps paint the picture of things fitting together in an intuitive way, recovering that initial discontinuity as continuity. And in the case of Niconico, this effect coincides with the sociality of anonymous communication to allow users to remain invisible as individuals even while participating in more spectacular forms of text production (such as *danmaku* and comment art).

This is also part of the historical significance of asynchronous media design in the contemporary moment. Online media, as telephones, radio, and television before them, allow for a flexible sense of simultaneity that can reach a large number of bodies and across vast reaches of space. This is part of why the network has become such a powerful emblem of late twentieth-century and early twenty-first-century life, in some ways even representing that expectation of immediacy and simultaneity through media communication infrastructures. With that demand for immediate access and response come new pressures and responsibilities, with the latest communication technologies offering as much of a tether to professional and social obligations as they do the pleasures of new forms of mobility and personal lifestyles. But this sense of connection isn't always linear or clean, and the recovery of that experience of "real time" and simultaneity between users is where asynchronous media design comes in. Media interfaces such as the comment feed on Niconico help recover the desire for connectivity that network society instills, preserving both the atomization of how individuals use media at different times and in different places with the sensation of these different instances of use being as if simultaneous to one other. This control over time through media can perhaps be connected to the emergence of "time-shifted" media such as video and cassette-based media, which also cater to individual use over public or communal experiences, such as a film projection.[20]

The significance of media temporalities has long been observed, since late nineteenth-century and early twentieth-century technologies (cinema in particular), and we can perhaps detect a similar social and cultural attention given to time through how it is being represented and experienced in visual technologies.[21] It is too early to have the same kind of perspective in describing contemporary phenomena, but writing in the moment (or close to it) also allows for a sense of historical witnessing that offers its own valuable perspective. But perhaps another point to consider regarding this historical significance of asynchronous media design is how it intersects with the fragmentation of time and perception of time in contemporary life, an experience often related to the precarity of the present and changing expectations about work, livelihood, and leisure.

Perhaps, then, asynchronicity is something that allows for different types of anonymity to possess these qualities of spectacle and invisibility at the same time. It structures what is overlooked into what is attention-grabbing, changing the experience of how we encounter that dynamic through different elements of mediation. If one of the key qualities of sites such as Niconico is the ability to recover discontinuity as continuity, then asynchronous media forms are part of the apparatus that enables online anonymity to play between seen and unseen, by expanding those qualities to issues of presence and absence. Asynchronicity might appear to render the distinction of presence and absence (in time, space, and action) less relevant, but we can also consider how it transforms those questions into part of the lure and attraction of a media form.

## Framing the Scope of the Book

Given that this book will organize itself around broad concepts such as anonymity and asynchronicity, the range of materials it could engage with is quite large. As with other local linguistic, technological, and cultural environments, the array of practices that contribute to internet anonymity and asynchronicity in Japan are quite diverse. That said, the materials that will be analyzed in this book are comparatively limited and will only survey a small portion of possible materials—those that feature rapid-fire waves of electronic text.

The Japanese origins of textually cacophonous media must also be acknowledged. Japan usually occupies a comparatively marginal position in the popular imagination of internet media culture, at least for English-speaking audiences.[22] Yet, to begin with a bit of a provocation, perhaps we can (and should) consider Japan as one of the centers of contemporary media culture.[23] This isn't the same as naming it as the sole center of media but rather an attempt to acknowledge the multitude of centers and registers in which they operate and orbit.[24] I don't mean for this to refer exclusively to regional centers of media culture either, although those are surely relevant. After all, Chinese-language video-sharing and streaming sites such as AcFun, Mio Mio, and Bilibili feature Japanese animation, game, and voice-synthesizer videos as a significant portion of their content but have also borrowed liberally from the interface design of Niconico and its commenting system. Even the English-language picture board 4chan was built using code taken from a Japanese site, Futaba Channel, and initially grew out of a subforum on Something Awful focusing on popular media from Japan.[25] And this is to say nothing of the influence of Japanese media on early listserv culture, which has in many ways continued to define internet-centric media in the English-language realm through the persistence of fandom and boutique consumer identities as the organizing principles for many online communities. That being said, these traces of Japanese media are usually invisible to ordinary users, which perhaps suggests an additional quality of being overlooked and allows for users to feel like questions of identity can be put aside in an unproblematic way, even as they affirm alternative categories of identity through the media they consume together and the cultural rhetoric of belonging and exclusion that arise in those spaces.

What it means to be a center for online media is therefore relatively flexible and undetermined as a concept. It can describe the literal appropriation of code and application design but also extend to cultural forms as a kind of style or mode of self-presentation. Both suggest a movement or mobility in media culture, one that is perhaps "in orbit" but not tethered. Perhaps, then, Japan as a center of orbit is less significant than "Japan" as what circulates and what organizes the act of circulation. "Center" is therefore subject to instability, even as the issue of centrality suggests a form of continuity. Relatively minor examples can also demonstrate the persistence of "Japan" circulating in contemporary internet culture. This can include the use of looped GIF animations and manipulated pop music tracks in Future Funk YouTube videos, which adapt eighties pop culture from Japan to the Vaporwave style of lo-fi and retro remixes and samplings.[26] But it can also encompass the mixing of Japanese media with anonymous self-presentation, such as the use of anime girl avatars by Twitter users participating in the Gamergate outburst of 2014, or even the popularity of video streamers posing as Vtubers (i.e., using face-tracking applications to appear on camera as an *anime* character). This use of Japan-sourced images and media speaks to a kind of masquerade in which anonymous users can recognize each other and reproduce the same rhetorical forms in an environment of aggressive antagonism. But it also conflates the fantasy of Japan as a cultural space "unmarked" by difficult questions of identity, obscuring gender or ethnicity in favor of simply the consumer identity of "gamer." For many participants in Gamergate and its related campaigns, "Japan" served as a fantasy of living without feminism (one of the primary targets of Gamergate's most vocal members), of not having to worry about political questions of identity or representation, and simply enjoying a mobile, neoliberal sense of self defined by acts of consumption. Images from and of Japan became part of the language for expressing and representing this kind of identity, even as many of its adopters refused "identity" in social and political life. This in turn speaks to the role that Japan has played in providing an imaginary utopia of what successful capitalistic expansion should look like for many parts of gamer and fandom cultures around the world, something we can observe in images and media produced in Japan, but also how those images have been recontextualized and adapted in locally produced visual culture.

This book focuses on media forms and practices that reached or were approaching a certain peak of activity between 2006 and 2014. Niconico debuted in late 2006, providing something of an extension for the burgeoning internet culture that had been developing out of 2channel in the preceding half a decade. Niconico combined the "runaway" writing cultures already common to text and image boards in Japan with online video, intensifying the aesthetic of barrage while also making online media more commercially attractive to mainstream media producers. Furthermore, Chinese language spin-offs of Niconico began appearing almost immediately (AcFun in 2007 and Bilibili in 2010), leading to the regional expansion of text-added video style. As such, this time period captures both the birth and initial transformations of *danmaku*-style media and precedes the rise in popularity of non-anonymous services such as Facebook and Instagram in Japan, which, while never replacing anonymous media, have had an impact on how internet culture has developed in the mid to late 2010s and beyond. Outside of that gradual shift toward non-anonymous social media, many of the media platforms being discussed also underwent significant transformations following that time. This includes the sudden change in ownership of 2channel in early 2014, with founder Nishimura Hiroyuki losing control of the site to American Jim Watkins, as well as the corporate mega-alliance formed between Dwango (the owners of Niconico) and Kadokawa during the fall of 2014.[27] The demise of 2channel's in 2017, when the site was permanently shut down, rounds out this narrative. The narrow historical focus is perhaps best demonstrated by bookending the anecdote about the protesters gathering outside of

Fuji TV's Odaiba campus during the summer of 2011 with discussion of the United States of Odaiba event held at the same location the following summer, as will appear in the conclusion.

## Chapter Breakdown

Chapter 1, "Animating Writing," explores the relationship between unattributed writing and pseudo-synchronous representations of time in the comment feed of Niconico. These issues are discussed in relation to deliberate mistyping, orthographic play, and redundant captioning. Through these topics this section serves as an introduction to some of the aesthetic forms associated with anonymous media platforms, but it also provides a comprehensive explanation of how the theoretical project of the book connects to a particular object and set of practices. Additional topics such as deviant script, network aesthetics, and polyphonic clutter are also raised to clarify and expand on the different styles of text-production that appear on Niconico and relate them to issues of anonymous communication and asynchronous media usage. Drawing on Hamano Satoshi's notion of "pseudo-synchronicity" in online media platforms, this chapter approaches acts of reading and writing on Niconico as practices of performative animation that enact counterintuitive modes of recognition in meaning and form.

Chapter 2, "Characters of Language," continues the discussion of electronic text and its connection to alternative forms of meaning and social connection in contemporary East Asian media. The chapter begins with a discussion of the "toyification" of language in electronic text and proceeds to discuss the defacement of images by electronic text. The discussion of "comment art" pairs it with other forms of nonsensical language in online media, especially in terms of how those practices relate to popular TV comedy in Japan. This includes routines of deliberate mishearing (*soramimi*), in which users will mistranslate speech to produce absurd forms of dissociative meaning. This is rounded out by an explanation of comment art on Niconico. These are simple images entered into the comment feed that are meant to supplement the video image by adding new cartoon-like icons made from blocks of color and simple shapes.

"Repertoire and Accumulation," the third chapter, expands on the aesthetics of accumulation in online media by considering it as part of a dynamic of deletion, acceleration, and storage. The instability of media form and content is stressed over unity of design but shifts the focus away from questions of the digital to consider how ordinary users of 2chan and Niconico aggravate the inherent impermanence of online media through routines of repetition and acceleration of use. I continue my engagement with Hamano Satoshi's work on experiences of time in online media, now turning to his notion of online festival (*matsuri*) culture and its associated sensations of intensity and acceleration in writing brought about by the impermanence of internet media. Suzuki Kensuke's work on "runaway" text production on 2channel is also used to expand on Hamano's model, which is considered in terms of how new notions of temporality emerge through the interface of sites such as 2channel and Niconico.

The impermanence of online media is discussed further in chapter 4, "Copying, Collecting, and Copyright." Here the focus shifts away from electronic text and toward internet video storage. This acts partially to extend previous discussions of the relationship between television and online media in East Asia, but it also expands on those discussions by demonstrating not only how Chinese-language video sites are used as a pseudo-archive for television programs produced in Japan but also how commercial media production in East Asia increasingly simulates the aesthetic design and interface effects of online video. These provide additional perspectives for analyzing the relationship between accumulation and deletion in digital media. That connection is in turn framed as part of a larger discussion of how anonymous writing in online media represents a shift away from individual authorship to distributed, fragmentary notions of authorship.

Niconico remains the focus of chapter 5, "Scripted Laughter," although it now shares the spotlight with YouTube and the streaming site Twitch.tv. Here the focus is on "let's play" video recordings of console and computer games that have been uploaded to video-sharing sites. These have become a major part of contemporary game and online media culture and industries but have not been systematically addressed in scholarship. This section offers a comprehensive introduction to this type of video media alongside a critical analysis that focuses on how audience's respond to images of failure and play. This section also functions as a shift toward game media as the center of analysis and a more deliberately emphasized comparative approach, looking at Japanese-language videos made on Niconico and YouTube alongside English-language examples on YouTube and Twitch. The conceptual approach for this chapter is strongly informed by Kitada Akihiro's writing on variety television in Japan and the way he connects television audiences with contemporary internet culture through the concept of irony. Kitada's model of ironic spectatorship in 1980s variety shows provides a basis to think about "let's play" videos in terms of comedic performance, audiovisual redundancy, and audience engagement with images of failure. The continuity of audience laughter these videos share with variety television is further explored through elements such as the voice-over narration of the player and the comments of other users, all of which contribute to the experience of watching as if together with a present and active audience.

*Textual Cacophony* ends with a bookend to the anecdote that opens the introduction, returning to Fuji Television's Odaiba campus one year after the anti-Korean protests that grew out of social media antagonism. This time the focus is on the way that asynchronicity and latency in online media can lead to acts of patience between users, who wait for others to "catch up" and share the same experience as they. It uses an event at Fuji TV's annual celebration in 2012 and the latency of streams on Twitch.tv to discuss the social component of asynchronous media, offering a final perspective on how users recover discontinuity as a way of experiencing media as if together in person and shared between individuals.

This book demonstrates the ways that electronic text and video media appear together on different sites and across applications, but it also considers concepts such as anonymity and asynchronicity in order to further question the relation of online media to social life today more generally. I don't expect this book to be the final word, but I hope it contributes usefully to the ongoing conversation about online media in film and media studies. I hope too that it introduces readers to examples from Japan that can help raise new questions for the study of contemporary media more broadly

# 1
# ANIMATED WRITING

The transformation of a still image into one that moves is a common way of understanding animation. This is often related to the perception of agency in such images, which seem to come to life with a will of their own, as with cartoon characters from cel-based animation.[1] This chapter will draw on a notion of animation to offer an analytic explanation of the expressive dimensions of electronic text in Japanese language social media. This will help to understand how the figural properties of electronic text gesture toward image-like modes of expression, becoming less dependent on conventional forms of denotational meaning and more like other forms of visual culture. But this concept of animation also describes the ways writing and, by extension, reading gain new temporal dimensions through their incorporation into moving-image media. Animation can therefore provide a conceptual frame for considering how issues of agency and expression in anonymous media coincide with asymmetrical experiences of time, contributing to a networked form of media sociality in addition to an aesthetic mode of expression.

This intersection between the figural and temporal dimensions of animated writing is also part of a more general shift in how image and text converge in digital media. This is doubly so in the case of video media using waves of electronic text in creative and dizzying ways. This is not, however, merely a question of visual technology or the digital. There is also a significant social component in how ordinary users engage with the animating potential of text-production forms to construct "deviant" script forms and express networked identities that shift the priority of representation away from the individual and toward the aggregate. The social dimensions of visually cacophonous media such as Niconico represent a new perspective on animation, which is traditionally associated with nonparticipatory media. These links between the movement of images, the synthetic temporality of media forms, and expression of agency in writing are where our understanding of animation will be focused.

The figural component of animated writing provides a necessary starting point. There are many forms of deviant script in East Asian language internet media. Focusing specifically on Japan for the moment, the popular message board 2channel features many instances of nonstandard language use that can appear obscure or even unreadable to a general audience due to the volume of seemingly incorrect character selections and grammatical conjugations. This includes an abundance of apparent mistyping of Chinese ideographs (*kanji*) in which nonstandard characters are used. At first glance we might be tempted to attribute this kind of writing to careless typing or autocorrected character selection through the keyboard IME (input method editor) typing system. "Netspeak" (or "netlish") has often been criticized for its perceived debasement of language, whether for the excessive use of abbreviations and shorthand, the mixing of alphabetic and algorithmic character sets, or its "vacuous" content.[2]

However, there also seems to be a semi-consistent use of some of these nonstandard forms of expression, and the online communities that form around sites such as the message board 2channel also appear to be able to communicate through this mode of writing despite the difficulties that accompany the use of nonstandard characters and wordplay. This is because many of these techniques are used frequently enough to develop into conventions that audiences learn how to recognize and reproduce.[3] Much of the mistyping can be understood by reading for phonetic sound rather than the choice of ideograph character, while others are understood through the orthographic proximity of characters from different alphabets. In other words, they engage multiple forms of linguistic content at the same time, conflating acts of reading and speaking as part of the same process.[4] These practices raise questions about what type of vision these "orthographic cues" infer and, more broadly, how it relates to questions of translation (Jaffe and Walton 2000, 575). This mixing of expressive registers across phonetic sound and orthographic design marks an important instance of the aesthetics of cacophony in media forms such as 2channel and Niconico.

Answering these questions concerning electronic text, expressivity, and opacity will be the goal of this chapter, which will serve as an introduction to how to analyze and understand this type of cacophonous media and its ambivalent forms. However, returning to the above-mentioned example of 2channel, the user-made text on that site is static. As such, while it perhaps provides a useful case for thinking about the figural component of new media writing and deviant script forms, it does not readily speak to the temporal dimensions of how writing and images interact through movement. 2channel has had an enormous influence in how anonymous writing forms have developed in Japanese-language internet media (Steinberg, 2019, 193), so it will remain a point of reference throughout this chapter (and will be discussed at greater length in chapters 3 and 4). But in continuing the focus on movement and animation in electronic text, this chapter will analyze some of the practices of text production and reading that appear in the comment feed on the Japanese-language video-sharing site Niconico as well as its Chinese-language derivatives such as AcFun and Bilibili. Unlike on 2channel, the user-made text on these platforms moves alongside the video images that populate the site, scrolling across the screen in a steady stream. The convergence of moving text with deviant scripts is where we will find a new perspective to consider the role of animation in contemporary media culture.

In exploring the relationships between animation, electronic text, and network sociality, this chapter will begin with an explanation of the aesthetic interface of *danmaku*-style video sites, then progress to analyze how users employ figural modes of writing in a media architecture of anonymity and asynchronicity. The chapter will provide a guide to understanding this type of cacophonous media and the way language is used in it. This will in turn provide a background for chapter 2, which will be dedicated more to the relationships between opacity, identity, and online culture in text-laden Japanese video.

## The Feeling of Time

Niconico has been one of the most popular websites in Japan since its creation.[5] It is also the originator of the *danmaku* or "barrage" style of video-text integration that has become popular in East Asian internet media.[6] In contrast to globally known platforms such as YouTube, the site has often required a permanent account in order to log on and watch videos, but many forms of communication that take place on the site (such as leaving comments on videos) are unattributed to individual users. Users of the site can upload, watch, bookmark, and comment on videos. Social media functions such as the ability to join communities based around mutual interests, give videos and comments "likes," and follow news are also integrated into the site. A wide variety of categories of user-created content, media mash-up collaborations, and commercial and semi-commercial videos are hosted by the site. In this sense Niconico is similar to other video-sharing services such as FC2, Daily Motion, and Youku.

However, even with those shared qualities in basic architecture, Niconico has a distinct atmosphere and modes of participation due to the orientation of its user-base toward media such as anime, games, and popular music. For example, the site has had a strong association with music video montage aesthetics and amateur performance videos for most of its existence. Among the most popular and characteristic of these are collaboratively produced music videos that use Vocaloid voice-synthesizer software to perform original music and remixed covers of existing songs. The virtual-idol Hatsune Miku is perhaps the representative image of this semi-collaborative aesthetic and social mode of production that Niconico has fostered.[7] The amateur performance category, in which a user imitates a favorite song or routine and then submits his or her recording for the rest of the community to respond, has also developed a large following ("I tried to dance it," "I tried to sing it," etc.). Some of these videos have been uploaded to YouTube and other video-hosting sites by fans, which has helped spread the cultural presence of Niconico beyond its core user base in Japan. As previously mentioned, Chinese-language websites such as Bilibili and AcFun have also followed the basic design of Niconico's comment feed and emphasis on certain forms of popular culture (such as *anime* and Vocaloid videos), providing another form of the geographic expansion of barrage-style media in East Asia.[8]

Niconico launched in December 2006 and quickly became one of the most frequently visited and influential internet sites for Japanese users. By some counts as many as one out of three Japanese in their twenties were considered to be a regular visitor to the site throughout the 2010s.[9] Niconico originally catered to followers of subcultural media through the focus on anime, Vocaloid songs performed by a sampled, synthesized voice, and video games. However, since 2010 Niwango (the company that manages the site) has made an effort at reaching a more mainstream audience by expanding its brand to include things like live talk shows, performances with celebrities from other popular media, and mobile phone applications to make the site viewable almost anywhere.[10] This strategy of expanding their audience even included transforming a disco hall in Tokyo into an augmented reality (AR) public performance space that mixes online social communities with live attendance. The site received a major overhaul in May 2012, introducing a greater emphasis on live broadcasts (*nico nama*), adding social media elements (such as ability to like individual comments), and rebranding from Nico Nico Dōga to Niconico.

Comments made by users are projected directly onto the video as part of a scrolling feed that moves from left to right, somewhat similar in appearance to the news ticker projected at the bottom of the screen on cable news programs (sometimes referred to as a chyron or "the lower third") or film subtitles. However, in the case of comments on Niconico and related video platforms, this column of text can appear at different parts of the screen, not just the region near the bottom. The comments in the feed appear to float above or slide across the image of the video, on their own plane of movement but still part of the experience of watching a video on the site.[11] There is a default speed at which text will move and default size and color in which it will appear, but almost every facet of the text's appearance is otherwise able to be manipulated by the user who inputs it into the comment feed.[12] Responding to the commercial and popular success of Niconico, other video sites such as AcFun, Bilibili, and FC2 have borrowed this design and presentation, using an identical or nearly identical system for projecting comments over video display windows. In Chinese-language video sites, this style of barrage commenting (*danmu*) has become the norm, even for more mainstream sites (Li 2017, 235).

This form of commenting is also frequently described as lending a sense of "live-ness" (*raibu-kan*) to posting. This is due to the way text entered into the comment feed is projected to other users based on the point in time during viewing that they were input as opposed to order of input. The comments are projected to address the content of the video or respond to other comments at the point in the video's duration that they were entered. This creates a "feeling of time" that Hamano Satoshi calls "pseudo synchronicity" (*giji dōki*) or "virtual time" due to its properties of experiential simultaneity despite the actual differences in time between users.[13] The representation of time is thus synchronic even through the literal experiences are asynchronous to one another.

Users can, of course, easily recognize that these comments are not being produced by an audience watching at the same time as them. Columns of comments with information about when they were input are visible to the right of the video display and make this clear. However, the mode in which the text scrolls over the video image produces a composite of previous users' experiences of viewing and reacting that are then replayed in the present moment in a way that produces this experience of pseudo-synchronicity. That presentation lends itself to an experience of virtual simultaneity in which users *feel* like they are watching alongside other viewers. The way users recover a sense of live-ness (or "liveliness") through their production and reception of electronic text is a key aspect of how the ambivalent nature of this style of media is subject to a continual, ongoing reworking. This can make it feel familiar and normal despite its aesthetic and social opacity. The comments in the feed disappear after a few seconds as they scroll out of the frame of the video window, or, in the case of static comments that pop onto the screen like film-subtitles, they vanish after a similar period of time. These comments are also displayed without being attributed to users, so the flow of conversation or banter that can occur over a video image is not experienced as a legible conversation or individuals but rather something like a digital crowd or mass that builds on itself through repetition and response.[14]

To elaborate on this feature, what Hamano is describing as feeling "live" on Niconico is not such much a literal sense of immediacy or of being there in the moment but rather a kind of repetition and reexperiencing of time. This can be called forth and experienced at essentially any moment through the way the comment feed seems to restage previous experiences of watching with each viewing. As chapter 3 will discuss in greater detail, this is part of a logic of accumulation that is performed and transmitted by users of the site engaging with the modes of expression made possible by its interface. Hamano locates this sense of performing "liveness" for the user and audience in how energetic posting patterns in the comment feed that sense of acceleration as more and more users contribute. This builds toward a surge of energy and feeling of participation as the waves of text appears to run away (*bōsō*) like the rapidly moving threads of the 2channel message board. Hence the presentational emphasis on visual cacophony and the free-flowing mobility of self-identification on these platforms.

The accumulation of previous experiences of watching that have been documented through user-comments allows for a kind of "anytime/anywhere festival" (*itsudemo matsuri*) that can be experienced over and over again (independent of the user's location) through replaying the video and achieving a similar experience (Hamano 2008a, 221–24). Hamano contrasts this to the temporality of threads on 2channel, which are deleted after they've reached a certain amount of content. This leads to an anticipation of the thread's closing and moving on to the next iteration. Hamano finds a more easily related practice of time on the microblog Twitter, which he describes in terms of "selective synchronicity" that is performed as a kind of "style" of real-time simultaneous experience (Hamano 2008a, 205–6). What seems at stake in all three cases is a divergent way of experiencing simultaneity via electronic media. The ways that asynchronous experiences of time organize so much of the experience of online sociality is a one of the central concerns of this book, but for this chapter I will limit the analysis to Niconico's unique interface in trying to develop an argument about the relationship between the visual syntax of contemporary media and the cultural practices of online anonymity.[15] What will be developed out of Hamano's analysis is a model for considering the performative nature of how time is experienced, interpreted, and reproduced for other viewers through the comment feed. This in turn is also tied to the routines of disavowing individual instances of identification in favor of aggregate modes of social belonging.

## Polyphonic Animation

As described in the opening to this chapter, animation is often associated with the perception of agency in the moving image. This is often connected to the way cartoon characters move and act. Niconico's presentation of time and how users engage with its interface offers another iteration of how agency in media might be tied to a notion of animation, albeit with that sense of animation being tied to electronic text rather than drawn images, and with the agency of motion more readily associated with the actions of the spectator via their input of electronic writing. However, because the distinct instances of writing made by individual users are transformed into an aggregate sense of voice, the feeling of agency we can observe here is one that speaks as a network rather than an intelligible collective of individuals. In that sense, the intersection of agency with animation here isn't one of individual action but rather the sensation of an active body of users who cannot be identified individually yet still possess some semblance of identity through their association with the site interface and cultural norms.

Mikhail Bakhtin's use of the term "polyphonic" can prove useful in understanding this relationship between author and reader, as well as between individual and aggregate. "Polyphonic," in addition to capturing some of the more general properties of anonymous communication found in online media, can also describe the textual cacophony of the comment feed, a "discursive noisiness" that contributes to the "emotional opacity" of electronic text (Ngai 2007, 50). This sense of the polyphonic is therefore produced through both the layering of comments and the unattributed writing system the site employs. It is also something we can identify as part of the aesthetic mediation of the social atomization of contemporary life, and part of the recovery of new forms of belonging within those fragmentary forms of interpersonal experience. The disappearing into an aggregate social form is part of a fantasy of finding new ways to identify within a disintegrating social landscape. This is also how the ambivalence of online media is often grounded in (but not exhausted by) its relationship to actual-world social formations and identities, particularly in terms of how online alternatives seem to suggest a recuperative alternative to existing ways of being part of a social reality, which for some, feel increasingly fragmented. The postscript to this volume will discuss this possibility in greater detail.

Bakhtin contrasts monologic narration—a style that grants a singular, sovereign voice to the author or narrator—with a polyphonic mode that leaves a multiplicity of possible voices intact.[16] Although Bakhtin is concerned with literature (the modern novel, specifically), this chapter will argue for a related dynamic occurring in Japanese media such as Niconico and 2channel, which favor aggregate forms of membership and participation that suggest a multiplicity of voices speaking at once and over one another.

As noted, none of the comments posted to Niconico are attributed to individual users, and it is not clear how many users are participating in a single comment feed just by observing the messages being shown. Whether these comments are coming from many users or from the same person spamming messages over and over is therefore unknown. This is, more literally, why the unattributed model of commenting can be understood as polyphonic. On the one hand, this makes it difficult (if not impossible) to analyze topics such as demographics that participate in commenting, instances of interaction between users in the comment feed, or clear relationships of hierarchy of the site's users. But this type of textual expressivity is also polyphonic in how it mixes aesthetic registers of sound with writing through both the volume of text that can appear at once and in the creative mistyping that conflates phonetic and orthographic modes of recognition. In that sense, we have a chattering of many indistinct voices competing with one another but also confusion about how to regard even individual instances of expression due to their animating play with visual and sonic cues. That sense of being caught between different modes or registers of understanding and expression is one of the major frames for understanding media such as Niconico as ambivalent, and in a way characterized through its cacophonous figurations of electronic text.

Given that polyphonic dimension to Niconico and its derivatives, it is difficult to understand what individual participation or even demographic participation in the site might look like. Referring to the message board 2channel, Yukiko Nishimura has claimed that between 15 and 20 percent of visitors post messages.[17] We should not assume that Niconico has an pattern of active writing and reading identical to that of other sites, even in the case of a related site such as 2channel. That said, Niconico and 2channel use similar forms of unattributed communication and have, as Hamano has observed, developed similar cultural practices based around virtual experiences of time, energetic waves of text that users produce with abandon, and localized linguistic practices. Both sites also present us with a (non)representation of individual users that suspends indexes of individual participation in favor of a more polyphonic social environment with its own logics of representation. The intensification of displays of written text that seem to belong to the comment feed itself rather than individual users is one way to begin thinking about this kind of aesthetic. The depersonalized register of language in anonymous, barrage-style media therefore shifts the focus of the reader or audience from the meaning of expression or contributions of individual users to the medium of language itself (Ngai 2007, 50).

## Network Unconscious

Writing from a perspective adjacent to this notion of polyphonic writing, Azuma Hiroki has described the way user data is collected and incorporated into net media as producing a sense of a "collective unconscious." He analyzes this as a variant instance of political philosopher Jean-Jacques Rousseau's notion of the general will. To demonstrate this point, Azuma describes how the popular search engine Google uses the information it collects from user activity. Google not only collects and saves the information produced by user-originated searches made through affiliated websites and extensions but also begins to anticipate what kind of text might be entered into a search bar or what search categories might be selected by users. It accomplishes this by drawing on popular search results and link selections to develop algorithmic patterns of data and behavior.[18] Based on this information, search engines and toolbars make suggestions for what a user should search for by listing popular words or phrases that begin with the same characters or even fill in a word or phrase as the user is still typing. This is commonly known as autocomplete, and it can be a helpful feature in using such media. However, it can also direct users toward repeating the popular search categories and results made by others. This, of course, assists in Google's commercial aims for its products and services. But, more abstractly, it might also present a way human agency is being transformed into algorithmic functions that work on behalf of information capitalism.

What Azuma focuses on in his analysis of this feature of data collection is how it produces a visual and material trace of information collection from all manner of users of online media.[19] Data collection is therefore not something that we encounter as a passive element in our everyday uses of internet media but rather something that seeks to shape our experiences in using internet media. It might even represent back to us what we are doing with those tools. These types of practices extend to all sorts of programs, including even basic language aids like Google's Japanese-language input method editor (IME). This software tool allows users to type in Japanese when using programs like word processors and internet browsers.

Like many Google products, the IME constantly collects and analyzes massive amounts of user data and uses this information to make suggestions to individual users of the software. As such, while someone begins to type a word or phrase in Japanese, the IME will begin to make suggestions not only for character selection (how all Japanese IMEs work) but also even more elaborate suggestions of words and phrases based on data it has collected by scouring the web for writing that frequently appears in text typed by users.[20] This convergence of data collection and the autocomplete function is a case of network aesthetics in which human agency is visualized in a redistributed form. In the context of internet media–based text production, we might also consider it to be part of the visual logic of online anonymity in which individual traces of activity are deprioritized (and even rendered invisible) in favor of the generalized aggregate.

These suggestions do not force users to write in a particular way to make a given selection. They do not, in other words, automatically supersede the agency of the user who is doing the typing.[21] That being said, by anticipating what the user is beginning to write and visually representing that process through a manner that continually offers new suggestions based on what search terms might be most effective (which are continuously revised as new text is input), there is a kind of direction that can influence the user's actions and cause them to even mistype what was originally intended. This provides one instance of what transforming agency in a network-oriented version of the social might look like. The aid offered by Google's search engine can actually interfere with the user or, more generally, direct the user to something that they might not have originally intended to write or search for by constantly offering new suggestions to choose from. The process of revision that the Google search bar is performing on itself is thus something that users of that media may find themselves reproducing by revising what was originally intended in a single message. These visualizations of mobilized data collected by Google also serve as a way of representing the aggregate of users through the accumulation of their data. This is another form of network aesthetics tied to anonymous media but also represents how these aesthetics operate in an environment in which information becomes commodified by those very network systems.

This manner in which user input becomes visualized or repeated in information archives can also be manipulated by users acting in coordination. This is commonly known as "Google bombing." Google bombing is most frequently achieved when users enter information into a search engine or select a particular result en masse to cause the engine's algorithmic aggregation to suggest those results to other users. Whitney Philips has described how online trolls used this effect to force an ASCII art swastika to the top results page for Google's trends list.[22] It is also frequently used in online harassment or slander campaigns, in which some users will try to associate an individual's name with a negative event, phrase, or description. Returning to Azuma's analysis of Google, he notes that in June 2010, entering the word *otto* ("husband") into Google's Japanese IME and leaving a space for the next word would bring up a number of negative sentences to choose from. These included "I want my husband to die" (*otto, shinde hoshii*) and "I hate my husband" (*otto kirai*).[23] The manipulation of information archives in this way (which Azuma describes as "a type of game") demonstrates something of the persistence of human agency in network culture but also how some users will assert their own agency over that of others.

## Captioning Agency

Returning to questions of interface and digital textuality, the projection of user-made comments over the video image is not the only instance of animated polyphonic text on Niconico and its derivatives. The tagging system that is ostensibly used to organize videos by established categories (music, video games, etc.) or user-devised associations is another aspect of these sites that shifts the register of participation away from individual authorship to something more fragmentary and environmental. Many of these tags describe the content of videos, such as noting the type of performance ("tried to dance it," etc.) or the presence of familiar tropes such as cosplay. However, as Hamano has noted in an essay separate from his work on pseudo-synchronicity, these comments also often generate new ways of thinking about connections between individual videos and provide another space for creative types of communication and performance. For example, videos filmed outdoors and in public spaces will sometimes include the tag "pedestrians who can read between the lines" (*kuuki ga yomeru tsuukōnin*) to refer to people who unknowingly walk into the frame, see the camera, and then turn around to avoid becoming part of the recording. "War" (*sensō*) is also sarcastically used to tag videos that have their tags repeatedly changed, referring to the constant alteration as a form of "tag war." Hamano describes the way users employ the tagging system as "generative" because of how the activity of content creation is displaced from a more conventional mode, in which artists produce distinct works, to something like an environmental space of collaboration between users (Hamano 2008a).

These types of tags do not organize the videos or describe their content in terms of genre but rather create new ways of thinking about connections based on more abstract or locally understood interpretation of video content and the discourse of the site's community.[24] In creating these new kinds of relationships between individual texts, the tagging system troubles the notion of origin of creation and similar concepts in artistic performance. As with the environment of anonymity that dominates the sociality of the comment feed, this displaces the activity of the site away from the video creators to a meta-interactive interval of collaboration in which the video texts become difficult to distinguish from the discourse that surrounds them. The textual mode of communication thus becomes part of the media object itself, and individual representation or contribution becomes suspended in favor of a more network-like register of participation. This sense of ongoing production resonates with the continual recuperation of the feeling of liveness in the media and its ambivalent dimensions of interface.

The commenting system and video feed on *danmaku* sites is also not just a tool for communication. It helps users organize the visual experience of watching a video. At the level of aesthetics, there is a quality of dimension that structures how videos appear through the addition of the comment feed, dimensionality that oscillates between a flat, shallow plane and volumetric space. The play between graphic text and image via the moving comments also produces a distinct mode of watching that incorporates techniques of scanning and an aesthetic of density and motion drawn to the surface of the image. This relationships between the video content, the comment scroll, and their planar separation produce a visual experience that is complementary and not just a reduction of the video image to a canvas for users to interact within but also perhaps something like an interstitial space of captioning that does not necessarily engage with narration-like content.

As Miyako Inoue suggests in relation to the captions of photographs, we can then think of captions as providing para-textual, supplementary information for an image (whether narrative or explanatory), indexical not only of the image being captioned but also of the author of the caption.[25] This might then be seen as bridging the moment of writing performed by the author with the reception of the reader or viewer, which creates a sense of "here and now" of viewing alongside the reader. The virtuality of time and experience on Niconico can be compared to this in how the artificial sense of "liveness" in watching a video is actually a composite of multiple experiences that are added to a larger body of time and meta-interaction, producing an intense feeling of social and participatory viewing as more and more "productive" viewers contribute to the comment feed. Similarly, the anonymous nature of the commenting system differs in that it might be seen not as indexical of an individual author but rather as a productive community of users writing comments en masse. This again is how the feeling of polyphonic intensity emerges through the site's interface.

However, one difference between the stable caption of a photograph and the crowded, moving text of Niconico is the potential for obstructing the image with text and in overwhelming the audience's ability to clearly read or view the accompanied image. This is one way of considering the "polyphonic animation" of the way that users produce comments, which introduces the possibility of the viewer being unable to understand an image or string of text fully and in some cases even seems to court incomplete or fragmented understanding toward the relationship between image and text. The following section will analyze some of the ways that users of the site engage in this kind of polyphonic animation via the commenting system.

## Spectacular Opacity

If text moving across the video image provides one instance of animation in polyphonic, cacophonous media, the transformation of text through playful manipulations of the input system reveals another. The internet has proven to be fertile ground for all manner of subculture jargon, and the user-community at Niconico has for its part developed various forms of lexicographical play for commenting on videos and organizing tags in the site. A general "netspeak" derived from the message board 2channel and other Japanese language sites makes up the basics of this culture of writing, but there are also forms of wordplay tuned to the sensation of synchronicity of time and the movement of text across the screen. For example, a string of "www" is often thought of as standing in for laughter. This is similar to "lol" in English, with "w" being the first letter of the romanization of the verb "to laugh" in Japanese, *warau*. Another common response that appears in all manner of video content is a series of "88888," which can be thought of as representing a round of applause. This is also a pun of sorts, with the Japanese onomatopoeia for clapping—*pachi*—sounding very similar to the word for the number eight—*hachi*.[26]

Some of these forms of linguistic play can be found on other Japanese language websites and social media services, but the movement of text across the screen that is characteristic of Niconico adds a property: foregrounding the congruence in time between the moment of the comment being written and that of its viewing by subsequent audiences. The synchronization of a wave of eights or w's following a performance or feat in a video responds to the content more directly than a message board post or blog entry does. Fukushima Ryota has even suggested that because the comment feed is unvoiced, strings of w's do not in fact signify in a primarily linguistic register but rather mark the experience of time that the comment feed animates and expresses a sense of excitement (*nori*). He notes how adding more w's to a chain emphasizes the strength of the feeling of laughter, which resembles a kind of nonsense or lightness in how the site allows users to project different affective states (Fukushima 2010, 258–59). There are also many types of acronyms and modular expressions used throughout the site, and some of these also appear so as to match the appearance or content within the video (such as "ktkr," an abbreviation for *kita kore*, for "here it comes!" or "here we go!"), but here I would like to focus on the way that manipulation of the writing input system is used to suggest some of the ways that language use on this site intersects with ideas of image-oriented writing. What I am most interested in is the tendency to spectacularize the opacity of written forms and flirt with illegibility.

An explanation of how typing works in Japanese will be necessary before describing some of these plays on typography. Written Japanese normally uses four alphabet systems: roman letters (*romaji*), Chinese ideographs (*kanji*), and two sets of phonetic letterings, *hiragana* and *katakana*. As a bit of a generalization, we might say that *katakana* is used for loanwords, onomatopoeia, and for giving a sense of impact, while *hiragana* tend to do the "grammatical work" of constructing sentences, providing conjugation of verbs, and identifying tenses.

Ideographs provide the general content or meaning to word, and roman letters appear in many abbreviations, foreign names (of people and corporations/institutions), and, like *katakana*, providing a sense of emphasis. Letters from other alphabets such as Cyrillic and Greek are also occasionally used in some media (such as mobile phones) but not so frequently on Niconico.[27] When these foreign characters are used, it is typically because of their orthographic similarity (in some instances) to *katakana*.

When typing in a Japanese-language IME, one writes in roman letters, which then—depending on which alphabet is selected—shift to *hiragana* or *katakana* as the user enters text. When a word or phrase is completed, which is typically commanded by pressing the return button, a menu will then appear to allow the user to choose the ideograph or other characters intended to be expressed. Many words in Japanese use similar phonetic readings of the consonant + vowel phoneme, although these can have slightly different pronunciation. As such, writing a common word such as *kan* will bring up a number of options, including the ideographs for "feeling" (*kanjo*), the identifiers for South Korea or ancient China (*Kankoku* for South Korea or *Kan* [as in *kanji*] for China), or even the ideograph for certain types of buildings, such as a library (*toshokan*). Pressing the space bar will allow the user to cycle between these different characters (see fig. 1.1).

Despite this emphasis on writing, the kind of language used in comments on Niconico typically takes the form of spoken, informal registers and features many abbreviations, slang-derived substitutions, and plays on grammatical construction.[28] Other anonymous forms of internet communication, such as 2channel, adopt similar modes of address, but social media services such as blogs that require attribution (whether a pseudo-anonymous handle or real name) will more often use comparatively formal, written styles of communication. This isn't true across the board, but there does seem to be gravitation toward more familiar, vernacular modes of communication that simulate the qualities of speech in anonymous environments and away from those in which the writer identifies himself or herself and takes on the role of addressing a public audience or readership.[29] Some of the plays on typography on Niconico draw on patterns found in spoken communication, such as vowel coalescence and phonological reduction, in which a vowel in a word is changed to match another or skipped entirely.[30] As Alexandra Jaffe has noted, standard orthography tends to render the speech-like qualities of text invisible (especially when it represents casual or nonstandard speech), while nonstandard orthography can sometimes capture the "immediacy" and "flavor" of spoken language (Jaffe 2000, 498). And while electronic text doesn't exhibit the same traces of authorship that handwritten text might, the ability to manipulate character input systems and change elements such as color and font size allows for these "deviant" qualities of expression to operate

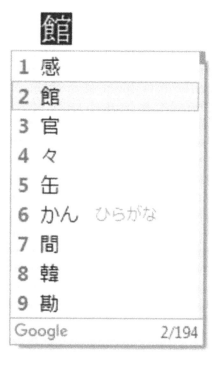

**FIGURE 1.1.** Google's Japanese input method editor representing a number of *kanji* for *kan*, including the one for "emotion" (top), "building" (second from top), and "South Korea" (second from bottom).

in the tools native to the platform and in the cultural dynamics of anonymous communication.

As described above, some of the more elaborate forms of wordplay that appear on Niconico are produced through the orthographic manipulations of character input systems. These typically don't change the meaning of the words but rather render each as an icon with image or pictorial content that partially displaces its linguistic content. It becomes something like a calque, when a word or phrase from one language is transposed into another in a way that preserves literal word for word meaning. This in turns provides a disruption of the act of reading, which becomes more aligned with something like decoding. As Jaffe has observed, orthography is part of how we learn to look at text not as language but as images (Jaffe 2000, 509). We might also consider an alternative form of translation, one that can account for the mixed linguistic and pictorial elements of the characters being used.

This mode of writing is based on deliberate mistyping produced through the properties of the input system used for typing in Japanese. The word "mistype" here might be a bit confusing because these types of text input that use nonstandard character selection are not actual mistakes but rather part of a semiconventionalized culture of reading and writing. This chapter's use of the word "mistype" is meant to communicate the courting of difficulty in reading and the way this form of writing encodes a certain type of identification with online communities. The engagement with the possibility of misunderstanding can then be thought of as leading to a creative space of producing new kinds of language and modes of communication and identification. Mistyping, after all, also calls for a kind of "misreading" that can infer what is meant to be communicated or alluded to through selecting the nonstandard character, and this mode of reading then becomes a kind of visual rhetoric performed by the community. This is also a significant point in that the activity of animation in these types of deviant script is performed by the reader, not just the writer.

As mentioned previously in the chapter, some of these plays on language can only be recognized by thinking about the phonetic reading of the character and then inferring the meaning, such as when the compound for "call and response" (*ai no te*) is sometimes changed from the character for "together" to the one for "love," both of which have the same phonetic reading of *ai* (合 or 愛, respectively). Other kinds of typographic play use orthographically similar-looking characters to the same effect, such as the word *kami* (神), which on Niconico typically means "awesome," being written by two other characters that, when combined, look similar: the katakana *ne* and the kanji for *mōsu* are written together to stand in for the original single-character word (ネ申). There are also cases where this style of writing is used to encode racist or nationalist sentiments, such as in the substitution of the first character used in the Japanese word for China (*Chuugoku*) with the character for insect or bug (*mushi*), which bears a rough visual similarity to the character for "central." Many of these plays on language originated on other websites, such as 2channel, but in being carried over to Niconico and altered further through the addition of the ability to render text in different colors and in manipulating the size of font, another layer of complexity in creating visual wordplay emerges.[31]

As with the movement of text across the video display and the sheer density of comments, these kinds of animated writing and textual aesthetics can disrupt the viewer's ability to understand what is being written through their movement between linguistic and pictorial registers of communication. They foreground the opacity of textual communication and embrace the spectacle of the figural image over clarity of understanding. This does not, however, mean that the pictorial content of text in the comment feed completely overwhelms or undermines its linguistic meaning. This kind of writing is still oriented toward communication, even if the register of communication has been radically transformed. This shift can also be found at the level of agency due to the shift away from individually identifiable authors to an aggregate, polyphonic mode. In that sense, while the individual identity of the author of each comment is obscured by the lack of attribution, the stakes of representation are also shifted toward this aggregate form of identification in which the cultures of the site become the site of identification.

With all of that in mind, we can understand this textually cacophonous mode of writing not just as a matter of producing spectacular and difficult forms of deviant script but also as encoding a particular mode of identification through acts of reading and writing. Text is animated in figural forms of play and spectacle but then translated back into language and meaning by the attentive reader. The animated, barrage-style of electronic text production is a form of image-based play attuned to contemporary visual culture and the social forms associated with online anonymity, engaging with aesthetics of being "overlooked" while also participating in new forms of visual attraction and image making. The linking of this style of writing to pseudo-synchronic media temporalities introduces an additional social element, one that provides for another form of identification that is mapped onto the abstraction of the interface.

## Different, Together

Before moving on to the next chapter and its topic, that of the character of language, I want to add that opacity conjures sensations of frustration and exclusion, while recognition typically infers something more aligned with a shared knowledge, language, or system of ideas. Both deal with the intersection of difference and similarity.

That dynamic is common to many forms of subcultural media, which are often directed to a niche audience and respond to mainstream institutions and the expansion of media markets through audience fragmentation. This is where many of the subcultural media forms that have been used in visually cacophonous video come from, such as animation, idol singers and other topics of enthusiasm associated with *otaku* audiences and consumers. This organization of media content—of subcultural forms being rendered distinct form the mainstream, often with specialized platforms for consumption and distribution—leads to increased fragmentation and, in some cases, alienation. Audiences and users are both separated from the mainstream by breaking them into smaller demographics but also have their identification with their niche intensified as it becomes shared within the demographic in a more intimate way (Kitada, 2005, 70).

Nonstandard orthography follows a similar pattern in that it signifies difference, not just in terms of language but also of value system and locus of identification (Heller 2010, 104). It entails not just an opacity of language but also a cultural system that values being hard to understand to those not in the know. Further, mistyping and orthographic play allow for alternative forms of expression in anonymous messages conveyed in electronic text, running counter to the privileging of speech between known agents in mainstream society. For a generation of young Japanese growing up in fragmentary social worlds, with little faith in traditional social institutions, this form of expression offers something of a reversal that grants a kind of priority to the social existence they find comfortable.

There is, of course, a charged political dynamic to these types of practices, which we can see in the opening example from the introduction to this book, as well as in the case of substituting the first character used in the word for China. But there is perhaps also a more general affinity between online subcultures and ideologies of resentment toward the mainstream. This isn't to say that media such as Niconico and its derivatives are inherently reactionary. Rather, they occupies a cultural space that is sometimes shared with those communities and forms of rhetoric. They also allow for sharing with other people who feel excluded from the mainstream and the vision of "the good life" we often see projected in those venues.

Lauren Berlant has described this desire to find acceptance, identification, and recognition as a "normativity hangover" (Berlant 2011). Ann Allison has in turn connected these ideas to post-recessionary Japan and the sense of precariousness that haunts social, economic, and political life for so many people (Allison 2013, 68–69). Orthographic play and its associated aesthetics of opacity don't have a direct connection to these sentiments—or at least not connections that are plainly visible. That said, the way textually cacophonous media trouble the very notion of being "plainly visible" perhaps speaks to the anxieties surrounding collective identity in neoliberal Japan, where fantasies of individual autonomy collide with realities of atomized social relationships and a loss of meaningful membership in institutions related to education and work. This style of online media and other forms of subculture offer the ability to feel apart from the mainstream that has failed so many people, but they also provide the ability to join an alternative social network that has its own set of practices. Navigating the opacity of internet culture, aesthetics, and complicated manipulations of language and images becomes one vector for exploring that alternative sphere, one that allows a certain degree of protection via routines of disavowal and masquerade.

# 2
# CHARACTERS OF LANGUAGE

The preceding chapter connected animation to electronic text via the intersection of linguistic play (in both reading and writing) with the types of abstract social forms allowed by asynchronous and anonymous media interfaces. The cacophonous agency in which individual acts of writing are swallowed up into an aggregate of users was also central to understanding the social dimensions of deliberate mistyping and related practices of deviant text production on Niconico.

This chapter will continue this focus on electronic text in online media platforms. The sometimes obscure relationship between individual acts and identities with the abstraction of anonymous, asynchronous networks of users will also be attended to. However, a greater emphasis will be placed on the "characterization" of how the text in the comment feed interacts with the images and sounds that appear in the video display (Nozawa 2013). This notion of characterization is meant to describe the process by which electronic text is used to mediate user identities in anonymous and asynchronous media, but also how the commodifying logic of popular culture becomes incorporated into these modes of expression. In that sense, if chapter 1 discussed text-laden video media in terms of how anonymity invites aggregate forms of social identity in online media, this chapter will focus on how the aesthetics of this media in and around Japan enter into a logic of characterful commodification through their reliance on popular culture tropes for producing patterns of meaning and association.

This chapter will approach that topic of commodified expression from two perspectives. The first of these is forms of writing that (re)introduce actual world issues of culture, identity, and media by creating contrasts between the images and sounds of the video with the language being deployed in the comments, which will often parody regional dialects or invoke qualities of de-nativization in speech. The second is "comment art" that uses the text-input system to produce cartoon-like images that modify the video image through their aesthetic overlay, creating a sense of animated augmentation through an aesthetic logic of diminutive iconicity. In both cases we can observe a tendency toward simultaneously expanding the content of the video via the images and text added via the comment feed while also reducing the logic of association through the emphasis on simple shapes, patterns, and language that simplify the meaning of these associations.

If opacity was one of the central elements of textual play in the practices discussed in chapter 1, the "toyification" of writing via image-making and linguistic borrowing (Tanaka 2011) will be one focus in this chapter. This will demonstrate how aesthetically ambivalent, textually cacophonous media incorporate images and ideas associated with other forms of popular media and culture in Japan but also how those processes are related to more general patterns of commodification in contemporary media culture. The concept of characterization, in which persons, images, and ideas become mediated by this sense of transformation into a playful "thing" (such as a toy, character, or image), is deeply connected to this tendency.

## The Toyification of Text

Tanaka Yukari's writing on text communication on mobile phones in Japan introduces the possibility of a "code of intimacy" in electronic media (Tanaka 2011, 9). Tanaka identifies how the use of script forms such as emoticons and nonstandard fonts or characters allow for written simulation of some of the expressiveness of spoken language. For example, writing in all caps can be interpreted as yelling, while using italics can infer a sense of marked emphasis or even sarcasm. As mentioned in chapter 1, the use of spoken registers when writing in languages such as Japanese is also quite common in online discourse, and this can contribute to a sentiment similar to what Tanaka describes as intimacy. That said, qualities associated with speech, such as tone and irony, are not easily expressed or recognized in conventional modes of writing, which can create a sense of impersonal distance or misunderstanding in things like texting or emailing. Users of social media will likely have encountered such misreading of attempts at sarcasm in written responses or posts, and arguments over such exchanges are common in venues such as discussion boards or the comments sections of news and media web pages. However, some users of mobile phones and social media applications attempt to achieve modes of expression that have a proximity to that of speech by creating visual plays on writing that encode similar expressivity.

These practices can be put into dialogue with some of the forms of writing we find on sites like Niconico, in two ways. The first is through the use of spoken registers of language in written communication, which enables a sense of casual association between users despite their actual-world unfamiliarity. The second is in the reliance on visual modes of communication to achieve new ways of articulating language events and their affective responses. In the case of using spoken registers of language, the kind of exchanges between friends or people who know one another and choose to adopt a more familiar tone is quite different from the kind of anonymous mode being employed on Niconico, in which users are addressing no one in particular but rather assuming a stance of familiarity toward the aggregate. What might be described as intimate is therefore quite distinct, particularly in terms of the scale of address. The attempt to use visual properties of text or to create images out of combinations of orthographic resemblance allows for a kind of coded sense of community that also engages in the reader's ability to recognize these forms of deviant script. The orientation toward the simulation of speech might be different than what Tanaka describes in mobile phone texting, but the way this kind of language use helps initiate a kind of in-group or community organized around linguistic practices speaks to a related quality.

The simulation of the expressivity of speech immediately suggests the sonic dimensions of cacophony, but, as we will observe, the use of image-like comments and messages allows for another form of intensified sensory address in electronic text. This is also something that, through its mixing of aesthetic codes, instills the pseudo-intimacy of online communication, particularly in the case of anonymous communities where the understanding of being a part of something is not necessarily felt through individual acts of participation but rather in being able to decode, recognize, and even reproduce those forms in a more casual, mediated manner.

To return to Tanaka's point, she claims that this practice of trying to achieve proximity of expression to speech in written communication is what led to the phenomenon of "dialect costume play." By this she refers to the way that non-native speakers of a regional dialect might sprinkle their speech with regional words or phrases that are associated with a particular stereotype or character archetype. The most obvious example of this is how Kansai dialect is often associated with comedy due to its use in variety television and the historical connection between Osaka and *manzai* performance (a style of comedy performed by two roles). A phrase like *nandeyanen!* ("what the hell!") might then be used by someone from Tokyo (or elsewhere) who is trying to perform a similar kind of comedic teasing of a friend during an exchange, which is mediated through an association of comedy with Osakan dialect and identity. Such an expression has characterful dimensions through its reliance of pop culture mediations, but it also resonates with a sense of commodification through its assumptions about meaning and value in a social order that the utterance is itself participating in (Heller 2010, 102).

According to Tanaka, this type of "cosplay" of dialect is also tied to practices of writing used in electronic communication such as mobile phone texting, which, like the above examples, use bits and pieces of dialect to achieve a sense of expressivity that isn't normally available or legible in textual written exchanges. The circulation of this kind of communication encodes the use of dialect with sentiments of intimacy and style, which then leaks into actual-world communication in face-to-face conversations.

Tanaka describes this as part of a "toyification" (*omocha-ka*) of language. By this she refers to the way that things like dialect become treated as an accessory to communication and expression, losing, or at least disavowing, their subordination to associations with regional dialect and becoming more grounded in the circulation of their use in comedic or character-oriented exchanges and performances. Dropping in a word of phrase from dialect therefore isn't the same kind of code-switching that a bilingual speaker might sometimes use but is rather more like contemporary discourses on *kyara* ("character") culture that relies on icon-like abbreviations of types to communicate a kind of generic form.[1] What is novel about this in terms of its status as a virtual language form is that it gestures toward a form of language not traditionally spoken by anyone but exists rather in the social order of the dominant. The characterful dislocation of dialect from geographical origin or local language community and transformation of words or phrases into accessories of speech or writing suggests a kind of language that exists only in quotation.

This toyification of language also intersects with the tendency toward disavowing actual-world categories of identity in favor of the unmarked, mobile mode of identification vis-à-vis the logic of neoliberal subjecthood, in which markers of identity become something akin to a style or fashion via consumption. Hence the notion of commodification, which here refers not just to the expression of value (which can be understood in terms of material, symbolic, or exchange value) but also the relationships between media, consumption, and identification. And while the use of region-specific dialects in electronic writing as a kind of added color is the most obvious version of this trend, the use of opaque writing forms such as mistyping and barrage-style commenting suggest other forms of shifting the stakes of identification toward the abstraction of language and away from actual-world entanglements.

It is important to observe that even though certain kinds of language appear to lose their subordination to the speech of real people, these language acts (whether in speech or writing) still exist in the economy of stereotype that has developed around dialect and geographic identity. As part of her analysis, Tanaka identifies the ways stereotypes feed into and are enforced by this kind of "virtual dialect," and she acknowledged that persistence of stereotype in the ideology of linguistic cosplay is important. Jane Hill has observed that this type of "borrowed" dialect or bilingualism also enacts a distancing of the speaker using a word or phrase as "color" through exaggeration and parody (Hill 1993, 154). These types of routines reaffirm existing social structures by continuing the circulation of stereotype and the maintenance of what belongs to the "ordinary" world of unmarked identity (the dominant group) and the "limited" world of culturally and economically marked forms that become objects for play (of the dominated group) (Hill 1993, 146).

Christopher Ball has offered a related perspective for thinking of the relationship between dialect and geographic origin. Ball argues that dialect (as well as honorifics in languages such as Japanese) are part of a strategy of encoding alterity in spoken exchanges, meaning that the use or recognition of dialect isn't simply about identifying regional identity but also entails negotiating the politics of in-group/outsider registers of membership between speakers (Ball 2004). This can also be connected to language ideology theory, which echoes Tanaka's point about the way stereotype is embedded in the casual use of dialectic for characterful expression (Irvine and Gal 2000

As we can see, the relationship between this type of virtual language and the actual-world identities and social configurations they refer to can be quite tangled and frustrating. In a sense these styles of expression represent how the expected personal liberation of online media (via anonymity but also the flexibility of media temporalities) might intensify rather than diminish the anchoring of virtual socialization and communication with those from the actual world, producing media as not a simple alternative to or escape from actual-world relationships but instead as a kind of restaging of their general parts and dynamics of power and meaning. In a way this type of virtual language is, as with the opacity of electronic writing described in chapter 1, a type of spectacle created from that ambivalence between the online and offline worlds, one that turns those actual-world signifiers into tokens of play without necessarily identifying or owning up to them as such. Within twenty-first-century Japan we can contextualize this dynamic in a highly saturated media environment driven by consumer culture, in which media literacy is itself entwined with a form of visual consumption.

The toyification of language is also at work with the various forms of commenting in media forms such as Niconico. From the creative mistyping that plays with identification of nonstandard forms of writing to the extrapolation of electronic text to image-making in comment art (discussed in the following section), the production of text on Niconico and related sites is often engaged with some notion of the toyification of language that extracts and appropriates meaning from other areas of cultural reference, such as popular culture. The image-making potential of electronic text is key to this practice, as it allows for ordinary forms of text to be repurposed and reanimated for these forms of written expression through their proximity to media consumption. However, the stakes of identification are also shifted, something we can observe through the anonymous mode of communication afforded by unattributed writing but also by turning language into the site of abstraction of identification, away from the individual and toward the aggregate. Toyification, like characterization, might therefore be thought of as part of a process of becoming, a process that has to be enacted by users through routines of writing and reading. And, as we will see, this process of becoming is often entwined in a logic of commodification of images and expression.

## Iconicity of Comment Art

"Comment artist" (*shokunin*) is a term used to describe a type of Niconico user who perhaps best exemplifies this tendency of toyified image making. Rather than writing messages in standard Japanese (or other spoken languages), they produce somewhat pixelated images and sprite images out of symbols and shapes in the character input system. These users produce some of the most spectacular examples of animated writing on the site and fittingly draw excited reactions from other users, who post reactions of amazement and encouragement for such manipulations of the comment input system. Messages rendered from solid shapes (such as squares and triangles) produce images that resemble cartoon characters, comic book–style motion lines, and simple representations of landscapes, objects such as fences and rocket ships, and fireworks-like bursts of color and pattern. One comment artist produced a simplified rendition of the video game character Airman by using colored shapes (see fig. 2.1). Many comment art images are borrowed from other areas of popular culture, such as game media, animation, and manga.

As with the ASCII art found on 2channel, these types of comments typically draw heavily from the selection of pictorial symbols that can be produced through special input commands or via copying and pasting from other sources. Musical notes, smiley faces, and other simple shapes are common examples found in everyday programs such as word processors. However, beyond the entry

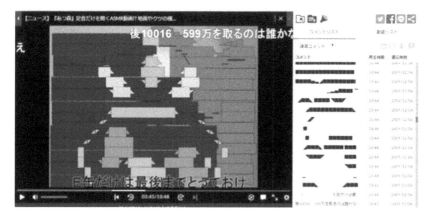

**FIGURE 2.1.** Example of comment art depicted the character Airman from the Megaman video game series. The window on the left depicts the video feed, displaying the comment art, while the window on the right shows the input for the individual comments used to produce the character's likeness.

of individual character symbols, comment art also requires the careful coordination of multiple lines of entry that are entered one at a time and have to be synced with the video feed. If done correctly, this will result in a loosely unified image that will appear in the video feed, playing over the image of the video itself.

As one might expect, comment art produced through these techniques is even less oriented toward denotational expression than even the most opaque forms of typographic alterations described in chapter 1. They in some ways aspire to be more like emoticons or similar types of image-making based on written text, although they require a much more complicated string of input commands and coordination of entries to pull off successfully. Like the alterations in typography discussed in chapter 1, these types of character manipulations are organized around the transformation of a character or letter into something other than its original function. Hosoma Hiromichi describes how the brief time in which comments are displayed in the feed on Niconico encourages *kigō*-like (symbol-like) commenting that relies on concise, image-like messages rather than complete sentences or statements, and comment art serves as perhaps the most extreme example of this (Hosoma 2010, 5). This type of comment art is particularly popular with music videos due to the way the comment feed can be made to link up with the soundtrack in a kind of para-synesthesia or to trace the movements of a dancing figure in a way that renders the choreography of a dance as a visual pattern.

Looking at a few examples of this type of posting can help us gain a better understanding of what is at work and the differences (and similarities) with the previously discussed examples of typographic play. These can also help demonstrate how, through engagement with music and popular culture, comment art operates in an aesthetic logic of image commodification that constantly augments, borrows from, and expands on of popular culture and media.

The first example is a music-related video uploaded by the user Daughter of Wota, an "I tried to dance it" performer. The video is titled "I Tried to Dance 'Sweet Magic,'" and features the user dancing to the Vocaloid song "Sweet Magic." This video features comments by a comment artist that trace the hand gestures of the performer as she dances, creating first a ribbon of visualized movement as she twirls her hands in the air. Then an explosion of dashes, asterisks, and punctuation marks appear as stardust from the dancer's hands and arms, creating a pattern of shapes that follow her gestures (see fig. 2.2). This creates an additional layer of performance through the comment artist's augmentation of the dancer's movements, which speaks to the mixing of aesthetic forms and materials that we can identify with textual cacophony.

Other examples of this type of commenting include the production of subtitle-like transcriptions of lyrics that appear and move to link with the singer's performance. One case, seen in a video for the song "Uninstall," features a comment artist producing colorful subtitles of the lyrics that are superimposed in multiples and pop onto the screen in patterns to match the singer's voice. As with the captions of dialogue mentioned in the preceding section, these are timed to create a sense of a textual echo of the spoken word, but the use of superimposition,

**FIGURE 2.2.** Comment art traces gestures and choreography in "I Tried to Dance 'Sweet Magic' " with ribbons of virtual glitter and heart shapes.

**FIGURE 2.3.** Song lyrics from "Uninstall" rendered in different colors and sizes, superimposed many times over, animated by the comment feed.

different size fonts for each letter, and movement and appearance of text across the screen also turns it into a visual display in which the patterns of movement, color, and timing render the writing as another kind of para-synesthesia (see fig. 2.3). There is again a sense of animation through how the comments move in the feed and how the characters themselves are foregrounded as figural images and not just language. More so than other users of the site, these comment artists highlight the comment feed as part of the visual attraction of the video and not just part of the site's social networking design.

This, however, returns us to the question of how linguistic meaning intersects with pictorial content and threatens to make it illegible. As swarms of comments pass over the screen it can be difficult to focus on a single line of text or area of the screen. Trying to take in the screen as a whole renders the experience from one of reading and focused looking into one that is kinesthetic: textual cacophony and a tangible sensation of movement and energy.

## A Somebody among Nobodies

There is a degree to which comment art and comment artists trouble the notion of a general sense of anonymity in which all users share the same nonhierarchical status. Comment artists are afforded prestige in the user community based on their ability to produce impressive combinations of shapes and symbols. Many will even make videos (often a blank screen throughout) to practice making new types of designs without interference from other users. In that sense, comment artists have a privileged position in the discourse of the site; although comments are not attributed to individuals, the role they fulfill is one that commands recognition in the performance community of the site. For example, while users do sometimes respond to other comments in their writing, comment artists are typically the only ones to enjoy much personal attention or praise (sometimes even more than the makers of the video and its performers), even gaining a kind of ownership or authorship of a video through recognition in the tagging system. This isn't to say that the identities of comment artists are known, or even that the work of an individual user can be traced from one video to another. There is, however, a sense of recognition of this general role in the site, so users who can perform this type of animated writing become something like a character-type in the discourse produced by their audience.

The status of the video as a canvas for commenting is also realigned by comment art. Colorful text generated via the comment feed not only decenters the video as focus of attention but also demonstrates the instability of each video as a fixed, unified object. If the way the video appears is constantly changing as new comments are entered, then its status as a media object seems to slip away, and it becomes a site of media performance. This tendency toward transformation hints at energy contained and expressed in these videos and their comments. In chapter 1 the ways in audiences engage with the videos via the comment feed to produce new kinds of meaning and activity was described as "productive." But they can also be compared to actual-world image-making practices such as graffiti, which, while playful in their use of color, shape, and appropriation of public space, also have the capacity for defacement via excessive alteration and modification.

Michael Taussig's writing on different forms of defacement has characterized acts of destruction of monuments, art, and cultural objects as releasing a "surplus of negative energy" that unearths knowledge, reveals mystery, and initiates a new way of knowing an object, person, or event (Taussig 1999, 5). There can be a kind of productive or animating force that comes with the moment of defacement in addition to the act of destruction. For example, the act of destroying a body as part of a funeral pyre is what imbues the body with sacred power and meaning. The constellation of practices and roles that appear to maintain these types of events are also part of this logic of productive defacement. But Taussig also describes how the destruction or vandalizing of monuments releases the energy that they hold in dormancy, which goes unnoticed in everyday life. This again is a kind of sacred energy that is often tied to the thing the monument or work of art is representing, such as the bodies of royalty. Taussig writes, "Defacement works on objects the way jokes work on language, bringing out their inherent magic nowhere moreso than when these objects become routinized and social" (Taussig 1999, 5).

The comment feed on Niconico can also be considered a kind of defacement. Comments, whether linguistic or pictorial, can distract from the video and cover it up, but they can also enhance and augment it through the way they are arranged by the users who write them. As chapter 1 described, comments share qualities with captions, but their ability to obscure or overtake the original moving image also suggests something beyond ordinary captioning. Hence the comparison with graffiti, which can serve as a powerful metaphor for thinking about the productive and destructive work that comment art and writing can do to the videos that they accompany. Comments projected over a video on Niconico do not literally destroy the image, but they both decenter it as the user's locus of experience on the site and produce a new, composite media form out of the layering of text over image. This dynamic and requalification of the image can help clarify how acts of defacement also open media up to new forms of interpretation, signification, and transformation.

Graffiti writing is, like comment art on Niconico, a curious meeting of anonymous writing and a system of author-based prestige in artistic form. Graffiti artists typically adopt pseudonyms to sign their work and develop elaborate signatures that borrow from other art and media. In some networks, being able to write one's name in hard-to-reach spaces also commands local prestige. For example, the graffiti artist Cornbread gained widespread attention for stunts such as vandalizing a TWA jet and writing "Cornbread welcomes you to Philadelphia" on an airport sign. The publicity and notoriety of creating flashy signatures, writing in outrageous places, or even writing over other artists work become the focus of many kinds of graffiti writing and the value systems held by the communities that practice such art.[2]

Tagging a certain space or object can also be interpreted as an invitation to write over that surface, whether it be a subway car, wall of a building, or desk in a classroom. The transformative potential in graffiti writing is therefore not simply tagging one's territory but also in turning something familiar into a new kind of writing surface. The addition of the comment feed to the videos shown on Niconico performs a similar function in turning videos into a surface for writing. The ways that users repeat the same kinds of messages over and over (even after they have been automatically erased from the comment feed) indicates how users learn to transform a video into a particular space for writing and for rehearsals of textual production.

Graffiti writing and commenting on Niconico are also typically impermanent forms of writing. As will be described in greater depth in chapter 3, the comment feed only displays up to one thousand comments at a time and at that point automatically replaces older comments with new ones, effectively erasing older comments from the video. Graffiti is subject to more deliberate forms of removal. The Metropolitan Transit Authority of New York City went to great trouble to remove graffiti writing from its subway cars in the 1970s and 1980s. Paul Pettit, the former general superintendent of the MTAs 207th Street yard, once asserted, "Graffiti is not art in any way, shape, or form. Art to me is everlasting" (I. Miller 2012, 7). Tearing buildings down also removes the graffiti that has been added to them, as does retiring old train cars. But graffiti, like the internet writing this volume describes, is not something we should think of just as individual acts of writing or drawing. It is rather part of a more abstract culture and an aggregate form of identification that exists in acts of circulation and transmission. In this sense, the removal of a single piece of graffiti writing does not destroy the life of graffiti. It lives on through practices of transmission.

We can even see this stance, how graffiti artists treat their own writing, in how established names for tagging would be passed down or even sold between artists, often adding roman numerals after the name to demonstrate its longevity throughout generations of artists (Stewart 2009, 28). Authorship is therefore simultaneously part of a system of prestige but also deindividualized to be the register of activity. This is, of course, also true with factions that use the same (or similar) tags in their graffiti. A related stance toward authorship can be seen in the use of copy-and-paste ASCII artwork on 2channel and the reuse of different pieces of comment art on Niconico, as well as the more general pattern of repeating the same messages over and over. Individual instances of destruction therefore do not erase what graffiti writing or commenting are or do, because they are part of a culture of transmission that is constantly circulating and being remade. Their archive is alive and generates an alternative form of identification that shares the production of meaning between acts of writing and reading.

## Double Vision

The shared status as language and image is one of the most significant aspects of electronic text production on visually cacophonous media. Chapter 1 discussed how users write in this style, but we should begin developing a way to understand how visitors to Niconico and others will read or look at this type of commenting. Zabet Patterson's work on Stan Vanderbeek's POEMFIELDs videos and computer screens offers further insights in understanding this relationship between linguistic character and pictorial image and the ways people may perceive barrage-style media. In writing on early computer art in which images were made by arranging letters, numbers, and other symbols, Patterson shows how these characters simultaneously produce pictorial, linguistic, and schematic meanings (Patterson 2010). She refers to this a "double vision of text and image" that cannot simply be read but must also be *seen* due to their status as both linguistic content and pictorial shapes and images (Patterson 2010, 245, 258). This is then not only a simultaneous production of image and language-oriented forms of content but also a form of vision that "reads" both registers as part of the same act of vision.[3]

The wordplay based on phonetic reading or orthographic resemblance on Niconico also troubles this distinction between reading and other types of vision (as well as conflating speech and reading), although with the nuance that it is also part of a social environment and not just a media object or other form of text. The strategies of identification employed by users are therefore more urgent than they would be with visual art. Furthermore, the comment feed is a discourse in addition to being a visual media form, which is why it is important to keep in mind the linguistic and communicative properties of such writing. Similarly, the characters used in this type of text production are borrowed from a linguistic alphabet (as opposed to the symbols of Patterson's examples), but they are being deployed in a way that disrupts the assumed transparency of language and foregrounds the image-quality of ideographs and graphically similar characters.

The technological processes, historical moment, and cultural context for Niconico are, of course, very different from that of the mid-sixties POEMFIELDs and other kinds of text-like computer art, but Patterson's point about an aesthetic of "double vision" or simultaneous signification can help clarify some of the properties of the orthographic alteration on Niconico that render text as having properties of an image or icon.

The way text is presented on the site should also be addressed. The use of color and different fonts and font sizes call attention to the image-like qualities of comments, but it is the movement of text in the comment feed and the arrangement of text around the experience of time where Patterson's notion of "double vision" can be used. The video for "Niconico Medley" (*Kumikyoku: niconico dōga*) provides a few instances that might help demonstrate how the animation of text through movement produces a kind of vision similar to what Patterson describes.[4] For example, when the video switches to the anime song "Uninstall" (which is an often used as the background music for videos), some of the commenters begin to produce text that moves to match the rhythm and the lyrics.[5] When the video transitions from the previous song into "Uninstall," multiple layers of the word "uninstall" written in roman letters fly by the screen, appearing in different colors and font sizes and moving at different speeds (see fig. 2.4). This style of commenting foregrounds the planar, layered aesthetic of the video display system and its visual syntax of the interstitial. As the song progresses, a cluster of the ideograph for the number three move by as the song's lyrics appear word by word, in a circular motion to suggest an unfolding or unraveling of the lyrics. Some of the comments are layered over one another to again produce a sense of depth in the comment feed. The performance concludes with the lyrics "I can't figure it out" (*rikai dekinai*) being written out, with the first character appearing in a circle around the edge of the video display and each successive character appearing within the next ring of the circle. The combination of movement of text and the emphasis on color and size renders the comments as images to be looked at in addition to messages meant to be read and understood.

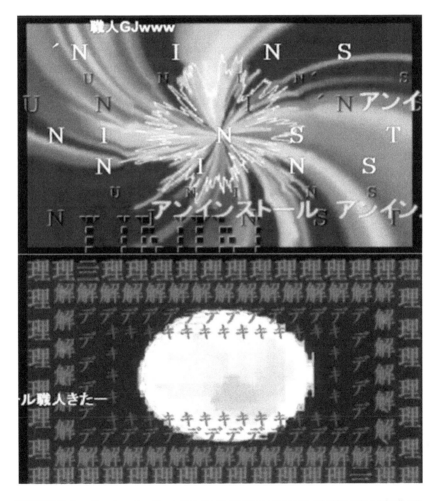

**FIGURE 2.4.** Two images from the "Uninstall" sequence of "Niconico Medley." The top image shows lyrics spelled out over patterns that create a sense of depth, while the lower image depicts a framework of moving text narrowing in on a center.

Patterson describes how the relationship between reader or audience and the media object can be thought of as entailing "double vision": reading and seeing at the same time. In the case of Niconico, the mode of vision is based not just on the reading of animated text but also of scanning and looking as comments scroll or otherwise move across the screen. We have tension between multiple interpretive processes: ways audiences might respond and ways the animated comment feed draw the viewer's eye to the surface of the image or direct him or her toward particular modes of vision. This again suggests a visual syntax of barrage.

Returning to some of the ideas expressed in chapter 1, this can also bring us back to Bakhtin's description of polyphonic narration in literature. Following on Naoki Sakai's development of this notion in his work on the cultural history of eighteenth-century Japan, this might allow for something like participatory reading in that the language is not reified in a sovereign voice of author or narrator but rather opened up into a space of creativity in reading (Sakai 1992, 26). In other words, the animation of writing on Niconico isn't just a property of mistyping or using nonstandard characters but rather of reading and looking in a way that can reconfigure the relationship between image and writing, or even speech and text. Along with the movement from monological writing toward a polyphony, communications on sites like Niconico can be thought of as moving from individual representation or agency toward networked intersubjectivity and meta-interaction. And this can also be considered a property of translation, while perhaps different from more conventional understandings of the term.

To return to one of this book's conceptual areas of focus, the relationship between sensations of movement and vision and reading might be thought of in terms of animation and performance. The dynamic between movement and stillness has become a productive point for thinking about animation in recent scholarship in film and media studies, and we can consider the Niconico comment feed with this in mind. The scrolling motion of the comment feed, in conjunction with the typographic transformations of text and use of image-oriented writing, animates text in a way that renders reading into a kind of visual performance taken up by the viewer. This sense of movement and temporal proximity to other users adds to the experience of watching. This returns us again to how the aesthetic of the site can be seen as directing users toward a way of seeing or looking rather than just reading.

## Performing Animation

Before concluding this chapter's analysis of writing (and reading) on Niconico, it might be in order to develop a more precise model for thinking of how concepts like performance and animation intersect with those of reading and writing. Thinking of typographic play as a kind of animation can help clarify this. However, in order to make this connection between animation of images and animation of experiences of time, it is also important to make a conceptual turn toward the relationship between animation and performance.

Performance has often been framed in terms of mimesis, identity, and an introjection of the social and physical environment toward the self. Animation has conversely been conceptualized as a kind of alterity, in which the self is projected onto the environment.[6] However, in her essay "Animation: The New Performance?," Teri Silvio questions the this distinction, looking to activities such as cosplay to consider ways performance becomes a kind of "self animation" through actions such as posing and lip-synching, which she sees as turning the human body into a puppet-like medium for embodying a character or image. She goes on to define animation as a medium-oriented projection structured around a "transitional space" in which "boundaries between self and world are encountered, crossed, and reconstructed" (Silvio 2011, 427). Silvio's essay is mostly concerned with characters such as video game avatars, media mix merchandise icons, and cartoons, but we can see also another kind of interstitiality in communication and online sociality in her notion of "transitional space." The remainder of this chapter will take this idea up in considering the comment feed on Niconico as a kind of performative animation in relation to ideas of alterity in communication, both in how patterns of typographic play highlight the interpretive process of reading and fragmentary nature of understanding and in how asynchronous experiences of time are represented as pseudo-synchronic.

Similarly, Laura Marks has noted how calligraphic animation of Arabic writing "shifts the locus from representation to performance" due to an emphasis on transformation and movement (Marks 2011, 309). In regard to Niconico, this observation is productive in considering how the transformation of text through typographic manipulation and movement can be looked at as a similar instance of performative writing and reading. More specifically, the foregrounding of language's qualities of animation through practices such as deliberate mistyping and production of sprite-like images suggests a mode of communication and interaction moving away from exclusively denotational representation and toward something like the performative or image-oriented. The way the comment feed allows users to watch as if viewing alongside others indicates another intersection between reading, writing, and performance.

This can also be connected to general notions of use and interface in media technologies and the way, for example, that IME systems vary greatly depending on the language being entered. Drawing on Marks's work on animation of Arabic writing, we might think of some of the ways that inputting characters in different alphabets can produce distinct kinds of animation and performance in text production. Marks describes how the lettering for Arabic changes depending on what character precedes or follows a given character, so that the process of typing a word or sentence through a word-processor input system produces something like an "animated movie," as the characters change shape in to match the new letters being written (Marks 2011, 319). The character input system for Japanese is quite different, but a comparison might help us think about how animation is performed between the user and computer.

Writing with a Japanese input method editor uses a phonetic alphabet that, through the process of typing out a word, allows the user to choose from one of the ideographic characters to match the word one is looking for through a dropdown menu or by scrolling through a series of options in the highlighted word or phrase. The mistyping described in chapter 1 comes about through a deliberate selection of the "wrong" ideograph: the user chooses a character with the same phonetic but a different denotational expressionIn considering the different processes by which a character is rendered or selected, it might then be possible to conclude that in Arabic-language character input the computer performs the act of animation for the user by changing the letter to match what is being typed out, while Japanese-language IME use performs a kind of animation by going against the system's suggestion for which ideograph to use. However, this might be better thought of as something more like a machine-affinity between the operator and computer rather than a kind of resistance to technology.[7] Thus, in the same way that the aesthetics of Niconico comment art direct vision to the surface of the image and suggest multi-dimensionality, the animation of writing in Arabic via IME systems directs the user toward performativity.

This is perhaps a more literal, practice-oriented way of thinking about animation or performance than what this chapter has discussed above. We can return to Silvio's comments on online communication to attempt to clarify what this means more generally. Her description of emoticons in internet communities serves as a good starting point for developing this idea of reading and writing as performance. Silvio calls these kinds of pictorial texts "icon(s) of general affect" that "remediate the pose" of activities like cosplay or puppetry through their reliance on visual proximity to familiar shapes, gestures, and the emotional legibility of the human face (Silvio 2010, 433). An emoticon or image macro doesn't express the emotional state of the individual typing that symbol as much as it expresses an abstract, general sensibility that everyone can recognize (e.g., "happiness," rather than the happiness any one person is feeling at any one moment). The register of communication is thus displaced from a desire to express the thoughts of feelings of an individual subject and toward a group register of affective, image-oriented movement and action. These become framed in this idea of the general that, like language, the individual has no sovereignty over language but can take up in speech and writing through practices of style. Mistyping that uses orthographic or phonetic substitutions of characters to render text as image-oriented on Niconico also produces a kind of "general affect" in which users negotiate the group register of communication through a particular kind of reading and seeing and engage in a mode of text production that is foregrounded as opaque and cacophonous.

This is another important point that Silvio raises. While performance studies have traditionally focused on expression or the production of meaning, the interpretation of performance is also an engaged activity. This moment of interpretation is also where we find the alterity of performance and communication, and, just as Silvio uses the language of "remediation" to think about various genres of performance and their intertextuality, here we can think of interpretation that misreads or mishears as another kind of remediation, in that it appropriates language for other kinds of use. The form of animated writing seen on Niconico cannot be adequately grasped without paying attention to the techniques of reading, scanning, and looking that users of the site must engage with, and these are all ways in which concepts of creativity in reading and interpretation are important in understanding how performance produces different kinds of meaning and sensation.

The meeting ground for animation and performance on Niconico can be found in Patterson's concept of double vision and a participatory model of reading. Opening up Patterson's concept even more, we can think of reading as a way of seeing, a way of translating or deciphering animated writing, or even a way of interpreting the pseudo-simultaneity of virtual time on Niconico that reanimates language in producing something virtual or network-oriented. It is in this connection between the ability to successfully read animated writing and read the experience of pseudo-simultaneity that we can find the mode of performance that constitutes the abstract concept of community on the site. Awareness of the comment feed's suggestion of an experience of time and the expectation of how language is used on the site contribute to a similar kind of pleasure of participation. Reading as a process of animation can be found in the transformation of orthographic manipulation and movement across screen surfaces, while reading as a mode of performance can be located in the kind of sociality a user of the site takes on in relation to the way time is experienced and how communication is interpreted. What is being performed, or animated, then, is an abstract idea of community organized around concepts of time and communication.

## Sense and Nonsense in *Soramimi*

Till now, this book has focused on the visual dimensions of online media in Japan. But we also should attend to the sonic dimensions of barrage, and the figural transformation of the spoken word into writing through synchronized comments is another key area to investigate in pursuit of the characterful qualities of language in such media forms. These can return us to some of the issues concerning identity, stereotype, and disavowal described in relation to Tanaka's concept of "dialect cosplay."

Transcribed mishearing of speech presents another way of thinking about how language can be animated to produce playful new meanings in video media, meanings that foreground some of the creative energies of translation. As with the examples of play on typography on Niconico and 2channel that deliberately use nonstandard character selection to initiate new ways of producing meaning, transcribing misheard speech as nonstandard text relies on a kind of translation that transforms speech into something different to produce a comedic effect through the dynamic of difference (denotational) and similarity (phonetic). The quality of translation at work in these practices is therefore not one exclusively of meaning or content but also of sound and rhythm.

This style of mishearing or misunderstanding speech as a way of producing humor has been a familiar trope in Japanese-language television comedy for many years. Variety TV in Japan has been a major influence on internet culture, both from an industrial perspective (such as the circulation of performers and staff between platforms) and in terms of how audiences make sense of screen performance and develop ways of identifying with media via laughter. *Soramimi* is one such form of media practice that has been adopted from television by online media culture.

The famous comedian Tamori (real name Morita Kazuyoshi) is perhaps the figure most closely associated with this type of routine, through the Soramimi Hour corner on his variety show *Tamori Club* (Asahi TV, beginning in 1982), where he appears as the MC with a rotating panel of guest comedians and commentators. This part of the show typically showcases mishearing (*soramimi*) for comedic effect by using a popular song with non-Japanese-language lyrics (frequently English or another European language) and then developing a bizarre translation of those lyrics into Japanese based on phonetic similarity. These translations are then showcased in a short VTR (videotape recording) absurdly visualizing what the misheard lyrics are describing. As with many forms of speech in Japanese television, the misheard lyrics are shown as subtitles in the show's graphic projection system. Typically cohost will introduce the clip, which will then be followed by reactions from the other members of the panel.

The "Mishearing Awards" special episode from 2012 featured a segment with the song "Got the Time" by Anthrax (1990), creatively misheard to render the hook's lyrics ("time, got the tick tick ticking in my head) as *kyabeji ha zenzen dekitemahen* ("the cabbage isn't ready at all"). This song with "misheard" lyrics was accompanied by a video showing flustered agricultural workers discovering that their crop of cabbage hasn't produced enough for harvesting. The translation is absurd, but the program commits to it by producing a nearly point-for-point rendering of the strange mishearing for the audience to enjoy.

On Niconico and other barrage video sites, this kind of mishearing is often used for similar comedic effect, relying on the aural proximity of sound between Japanese and words in other languages. However, since the video images are independent of the audience's comments, there is no visual representation of the absurd translation to go along with the new lyrics. Some videos will also reverse the pattern seen in *Tamori Hour* and feature creative mishearing of Japanese transcribed into English or other languages, even Japanese. For example, a mash-up music video titled *Starrysky IKZOLOGIC Remix* that uses samples from songs by performers such as Daft Punk, the Beastie Boys, Capsule, and Yoshi Ikuzo (the latter a very popular source for mash-ups on Niconico) features numerous cases of mishearing in its comment feed at different points. Users commenting on the video "translate" the Japanese call and response of Yoshi Ikuzo's "We're going to Tokyo" (*ora Tokyo sa iguda*) into aurally proximate phrases in English like "a soul let!" and "a you show it!" (original lyrics are "*a sore*" and "*a yosha*"). The same gag is repeated for the suffix phrase "*mo ne*"—"also don't have," which accompanies lists of commodities not available in a village—misheard as "money." In addition to providing a comedic mishearing, this gag also renders the previous absence of a commodity into a declaration of currency available for those objects.[8]

Another example can be found in a video titled *The Drummer Stands Out Too Much*, which was one of the first viral videos to emerge from Niconico. First added to the site in April 2008, the video shows a South Korean band performing a jazzy lounge song for a television broadcast, and its comment feed on features numerous routines of mishearing Korean lyrics as nonsensical Japanese. Lyrics from the refrain are misheard as *hanin da* ("a criminal") and *heijyoukyou* ("ancient Nara"). This example is also caught up in the fascination with (and hostility toward) performers from South Korea that is prevalent on many Japanese-language internet sites. The rendering of these performers as singing absurd lyrics resonates with Jane Hill's description of Anglophone speakers using "mock Spanish" in ways that use parody to create and maintain distance with the group they are "borrowing" from (Hill 1993, 147). The use of *soramimi* in this example can therefore be viewed as resonating with the frequently negative attitudes toward Koreans in online media in Japan; they are presented as de-nativized speakers of Japanese, even though they are singing in Korean. As with the dialect cosplay described above, this use of parodic language enacts a distancing between the Japanese-speaking audience watching the video and the Korean performers onscreen.

The role of misunderstanding or the possibility of misunderstanding in comedy and communication deserves further exploration. It is a matter of translation but also of identification. David Atkinson and Helen Kelly-Holmes's discussion of code-switching between English- and Irish-language speech in radio comedy from Ireland provides a useful comparison for thinking about fragmented understanding and the kinds of experience of community it can help initiate (Atkinson and Kelly-Holmes, 2011). As with many young people who live in Ireland, the radio performers and audience for these programs are not native speakers of Irish, so their command of the language is often limited and even on the verge of not really understanding at all. The use of Irish is therefore limited to very simply grammatical phrases or dropping a word or two here and there. However, even with this limited use and large possibility of misunderstanding, the use of the Irish vernacular also helps distinguish the audience as a kind of linguistic in-group that separates them from non-Irish-speaking Anglophones. This can even perform a type of border patrolling against exclusively English-speaking communities. This example is different from that of the mishearing on Niconico and on *Soramimi Hour* in that it is actually trying to avoid misunderstanding rather than mining that possibility for comedic effect. The typographic plays that appear on Niconico also typically do not involve switching between two languages or two alphabets in a single word, although the latter does happen occasionally

What these examples share, however, is the possibility of fragmented understanding as a mode or performance of community and the spectacularization of translation as not just a problem in language but also a source of new ways of producing meaning. This has more resonance with the way written text appears in the comment feed on Niconico as *danmaku* waves that overwhelm the screen and the audience's ability to read them. Just as the listeners of these radio programs might not understand everything that is being said, users who visit Niconico and read the comment feed can easily fail to understand the comments. Understanding the mistyping that appears in the Niconico comment feed or in the forum posts of 2channel requires interpretation akin to that of the audience that learns to understand the code-switching between Irish and English.

The possibility of taking pleasure in fragmented understanding and difficulty in communication should also not be overlooked. Theodora Tseliga's research into the romanization of Greek writing in emails that use orthographically proximate characters rather than the more commonly used phonetic transliteration finds that some users enjoy the challenge of the phonetic transliteration in how it foregrounds the process of translation.[9] For example, the word Αθήνα is commonly written in its phonetic transliteration, Athens, but orthographically it appears as A8hva. These two translations can each be understood by the reader who knows how to interpret them, but they operate under different logics.

But why use the orthographic version, which relies on a different style of association to recognize the romanized version as the Greek word? There is an assumption of informality that accompanies using romanization over Greek text in emails, but it is also part of a discourse on the use of loanwords undermining the Greek language, on the one hand, and methods of recognition and dislocating "Greeklish" from national sentiment and related ideologies on cultural difference, on the other. But to return to Hamano Satoshi's point about the festival-like culture of Niconico (which will be the focus of the next chapter), perhaps understanding is not as important as other kinds of sensations. In other words, affect can be valued over signification or can at least be a distinct pleasure. In the case of Niconico this means experiencing the sense of movement and meta-presence of other users through their comments. But the denotational elements of language in practices like mishearing (*soramimi*) can take a back seat to other aspects of communication. This is something that resonates with Atkinson and Holmes's ethnography of radio comedy and Tseliga's work on Greek email practices.

These types of productive misunderstanding relate back to the commenting practices of users on Niconico in a number of ways. The challenge of reading the comment feed can produce a sense of community or being in on the joke with others, but this happens by foregrounding the activity of reading in a way we can think of as performative and animating. The layering text that moves across the video image—and each other—also renders these comments difficult to read, which again asks us to think about the other ways in which users might enjoy this media. Not understanding, or partial understanding, social interaction should therefore be recognized as a distinct source of possible pleasure. Following this, the ways users adopt deliberate forms of linguistic play and communication that performs an opacity of not understanding can also be recognized as a type of community-oriented language use and as part of the logic of de-unified writing that flirts with the gaps between the written character and linguistic meaning, spoken utterance and audited word, and, most importantly, individual authorship over speech and writing acts. These minor instances of play in writing therefore speak to a more general decentering of individual authorship toward aggregate modes of circulation.

# 3
# REPERTOIRE AND ACCUMULATION

So far this book has analyzed anonymous communication and asynchronous representations of time in Niconico's comment feed in relation to topics such as animation, deviant script-forms, and the question of characterization in reading and writing. This chapter will continue that engagement with cacophonous text production in online media, shifting the focus to questions of repetition in impermanent media forms. As with the chapter 1 discussion of animation in writing, these topics will be framed by users' technologically mediated experiences of time, but we will now turn our attention to rewriting old previously deleted messages. This will include the prevalent copypasta aesthetics on the now-defunct web bulletin board 2channel, which will be analyzed as part of the practices and aesthetics associated with ephemerality in online media and, more generally, the "diminished status of originality" in digital media forms.[1]

One of the key facets of this discussion will be how websites structure and represent the duration of time for their users. The relationship to time that emerges from the automated closing of threads that reach the maximum limit of one thousand posts on 2channel and the practices of writing that users of the site adopt in response to this feature will one main area of focus. The cycling away of old messages posted to the comment feed on Niconico in favor of more recently entered ones speaks to a related dynamic of impermanence and repetition in online writing. This chapter will pursue these issues in relation to some of the questions raised earlier, particularly in terms of how they offer new perspectives on media ambivalence and the cacophonous aspects of electronic text in online media. The closing of 2channel and its subsequent rebranding as 5channel in late

2017 itself is emblematic of this pattern of deletion and re-creation, and that will be discussed in chapter 4.

The impermanence of digital media archives has been observed by many scholars of new media. Wendy Hui Kyong Chun characterizes the almost immediate forgetting or erasure of content in digital archives as part of the "enduring ephemerality" of their design, and she notes how this leads to a conflation of memory and storage (Chun 2008). But what about the ways users develop practices of use around the ingrained ephemerality of the media they engage with? The anticipation of content being deleted or the locking of threads on sites such as 2channel propels users toward a sense of acceleration in how they consume and produce this style of media content. The tendency to write with abandon and with a mind to disposability of individual instances of text production grows out of this mediated structuring of speed and ephemerality. This isn't to suggest simple technological determinism at work but rather to recognize the distinct cultures of use that appear around such media and how the practices that users develop that take advantage of or play into the particular qualities of each site.

This chapter will focus on the sense of impermanence in writing and media sharing alongside the impulse to repeat and recirculate previous examples of user-generated content. The conceptual claim I will make is that this orientation toward impermanence is related to a weakening in qualities of authorship in online media cultures. This is, of course, also part of the mode of representation suggested by unattributed writing and the aggregate social forms that users of anonymous, barrage-style media engage with. But it also extends to how the interfaces of these media forms suggest displacement of authorship into an interstitial negotiation between the user, the culture of the site they are engaging with, and the media form itself. As with the masquerades of identity that were discussed in chapters 1 and 2, this can be viewed as part of the requalification of the individual in contemporary network culture and the ideological forms of social atomization in neoliberal Japan.

Conceptually, this chapter also shifts the frame of cacophony as an analytic device. We have observed how aesthetics of obscurity and mixing of sonic with visual cues can produce an intense sensory stimulation that can confound some users and excite others. This chapter and the next one will turn toward understanding the notion of cacophony through the sheer volume of content and its associated sensation of runaway discourse and energy in online media platforms. This will elaborate on how this style of media can challenge its audience's ability to understand the images and language through traditional reading and watching, and it will further refine how that sense of cacophony is tied to the ambivalent relationship between online media acts and actual-world social configurations.

## Performance and Repertoire

In pursuing these modes of producing and experiencing different sensations of time, we should also requalify how the question of the archive might be approached as a way of describing internet media storage. While this might suggest prioritizing the past and issues of memory in media experience, it is also important to consider the present and anticipation of the future in analyzing how these experiences of time are felt and represented. Likewise, in considering how information is transmitted or reproduced, practices of performance, what Diana Taylor calls "repertoire," should be considered alongside more familiar tropes of preservation and storage (Taylor 2003). This can again emphasize the importance of how users interact with media forms like 2channel and develop specific modes of practice in engaging with mediated experiences of time.

Invoking Taylor's notion of repertoire in relation to online media that rely on textual communication might risk betraying her stated resistance to the dominance of the textual archive in how the humanities and social sciences think about memory and culture.[2] However, the particular instances of writing that this chapter will analyze are bound up in an inherent quality of impermanence that—to at least some degree—distinguishes them from traditional archives of print media such as bound volumes, microfilm, and engravings.[3] As we have seen in the description of orthographic play in chapter 1 and comment art in chapter 2, the forms of writing that the users of sites like Niconico and 2channel engage with cannot be explained solely through linguistic denotational meaning. Some sense of performance must also be introduced in describing the aesthetic and cultural investment that users make in these practices. This is where Taylor's work on repertoire and transmission is most helpful.

The tension between persistence and disappearance that Taylor locates in acts of performance (which she identifies as a mode of transmission) also shares much with the practices of saving, storing, and translating in internet culture that this chapter will analyze. In other words, notions of repetition and re-creation that appear in threads on 2channel or video comment feeds on Niconico all point to a quality of rehearsal that help to define the dynamic of time on these sites. These also become the routines through which users learn how to participate in these cultures of sharing, writing, and curation, which can be taken up and reproduced by almost anyone. As part of visually cacophonous media, these acts are chained together through repeated performances of the same writing. In practices such as copied and pasted writing or formatted blocks of text, the significance of the individual act of writing becomes diminished in favor of patterns of recognition and circulation in a wider field of repertoire. There is a kind of loss of identity in these types of internet "happenings" that favors abstract, aggregate modes of representation over that of the individual. However, before returning to the question of repetition and re-creation, I will introduce and elaborate on the concept of *matsuri*, or festival, as a way of thinking about experiences of time in these environments.

## Cultures of Time

Suzuki Kensuke and Hamano Satoshi have written extensively on Japanese-language internet culture and media. Both authors characterize online cultures of anonymity in Japan using the metaphor of *matsuri*. This term normally refers to a type of local festival, often tied to a neighborhood shrine or a type of wildlife, historical event, seasonal occasion, or regional cultural practice associated with the region. Japan thus has *matsuri* events that celebrate widely different occasions, although many share similar features, such as floats carried through town, dancing troupes that parade through streets, food and drink vendors, and colorful costumes.

Folklorist Yanagita Kunio has observed a type of social continuity that appears in *matsuri* culture in Japan. Yanagita notes that the limited time of a particular event allows participants to experience a loss of identity that can be re-enacted over and over when the *matsuri* is held again in subsequent seasons or years.[4] In other words, there is a dynamic that occurs between the temporality of the individual instance of the event and the more general culture of repetition and timelessness, both of which allow for a transformation in the scale of individual experience. As with Chun's "enduring ephemerality" in digital media archives, every action is one that is simultaneously forgotten and remembered, taking on new qualities even as it stays the same through constant repetition.

This chapter will not present a seemingly transparent connection between the type of *matsuri* that Yanagita describes and the way contemporary writers appropriate that term to talk about online anonymity. Issues of repetition, temporality, and loss of individual identity into an aggregate do appear in both cases, however, and borrowing that language can help to bring into relief what is particular about this type of media practice, hopefully without assuming any kind of continuity based on Japaneseness or similar national identity. In other words, the quality of *matsuri* that Suzuki and Hamano draw on when they use this term is as a metaphor, and they use it to write about online culture in terms of its orientation toward sentiments of excitement and activity. The casual sense of association or community that is manifest through participating in the same activities and the orientation toward performance are also relevant connections.

However, Suzuki and Hamano have different approaches and views of how experiences and performances of time fit into this metaphor of *matsuri*, with Suzuki drawn more toward ways of experiencing actual time and Hamano focusing on sentiments of anticipation. As such, a goal of this section will be to synthesize these two notions of *matsuri* to think about the relationship between time and performance in cultures of online anonymity, an intersection I will refer to as a kind of "happening."

"Happening" can be a useful analog to *matsuri* in that it expresses an event that has a fleeting quality and in which the participants come together through loose, casual associations. We can perhaps also link some notion of a happening with certain forms of performance art, although that term also implies counterculture and somewhat politically infused activist gatherings. In Japan happening is also sometimes used to describe the feeling of going off script in media appearances and performances, such as a minor error snowballing into a gag or spectacle that threatens to overwhelm the planned scenario. This is especially common in variety television. We might typically think of happenings as tied to feelings of spontaneity, even when this feeling is actually based on staged, rehearsed events. This sense of spontaneity is also related to a feeling of no one agent or author being responsible for the event. Rather, something seems to take on a life of its own, and the participants follow along in a way that feels or appears natural. The differences between *matsuri* and happening therefore may be slight, but this chapter will favor the latter to convey the seemingly random quality of the media practices described.[5]

Suzuki links the 2channel events he describes as *matsuri* to the experience of posting in "real time" as an actual-world occurrence is unfolding. He looks to online responses to events such as the terrorist attacks in New York City and Washington, D.C., on September 11, 2001, and the online bashing of Japanese hostages returned from Iraq in 2004 to consider the intersection between an absence of reliable, verified information from mainstream news media and the sometimes out-of-control activity of anonymous message-board commentators who spread mistruths or rumors while information is scarce.[6] This kind of demagoguery (or *dema*) in the wake of a disaster or catastrophic event has a long history that predates the internet and sites such as 2channel, but Suzuki sees a strong resonance between these practices and some of the qualities that structure and organize online cultures of social disruption. It is particularly through qualities such as "gag-like" (*neta-teki*) structures of communication, the idea of experiencing something in "real time" or "as it happens" online, and the cultural politics of anonymity and masquerade that he makes this connection.

Borrowing language from sociological theory, Suzuki relates this to larger questions of content in online communication, positioning this kind of writing (trolling, or *arashi*) as engaging with a kind of transmission that does not carry the same kind of linguistic significance as more conventional forms of communication. In other words, expressing meaning to an anonymous other is less important than initiating or sustaining a state of excitement (*nori*) among users who are in on the joke. Content—in both a linguistic and sociological sense—is therefore less important than affect in producing a sense of *matsuri* or happening in these kinds of media cultures. This is something that viewed in isolation doesn't project a strong political dimension, but, as we have seen, the fantasy of unmarked identity and playful association that often accompanies these practices often connects that type of *nori* to anti-mainstream (if not explicitly rightwing) conduct and discourse. As with other forms of electronic writing that have been discussed thus far, this can be connected to the reimagining of individuals' relationship between their online and offline selves and the online and offline cultural associations they participate in.

Suzuki notes that these are qualities shared among many general forms of trolling and shitposting, regardless of language or cultural context. In relation to internet culture and online forms of happening, he characterizes this orientation toward time as part of a practice of "killing time" through posting constantly and seemingly without investment in what is being written.[7] What is valued, then, is sustaining a level of excitement or quality of intensification in the act of writing and in repeating messages, with a general indifference toward the politics of the subject or the type of message being transmitted.[8] This points to how we might understand this style of writing as cacophonous, but it also resonates with the general framing of anonymity as disengaging from obvious political commitments or actual-world attachments that this book has presented, such as the anti-Korean sentiment described in the introduction. But this type of posting has a time status that is oriented toward fulfilling an experience of the present. This idea of the present and "killing time" while the actual event is still unfolding and unsettled also intersects with notions of anticipation, which is how Hamano Satoshi approaches these types of happenings, which he also describes as *matsuri*.

Hamano's characterization of 2channel overlaps with Suzuki's in many ways. For example, he notes the use of joke-oriented communication as a key characteristic of anonymous internet culture in Japan, describes the atmosphere of excitement (*nori*) as one of "talk without communication," and relates the manner in which users post messages and new threads in the language of time and flow (Hamano 2008a, 96). However, unlike Suzuki, Hamano describes the "runaway" threads on 2chan in terms of their trajectory toward being locked and disposed of rather than focusing on their potential of syncing up with the time of the moment or filling in the vacuum as information is still trickling out of other media. Noting the way threads on 2channel are automatically locked once they reach one thousand posts, Hamano's characterization of this sensation of happening (*matsuri*) suggests a quality of abandon that, in anticipating the eventually closure of a thread, essentially advances that end by pushing the thread toward its automated conclusion (Hamano 2008a, 84). This resonates with Suzuki's description of killing time by posting messages as an event is still unfolding and also with the feeling of cacophonous barrage in Niconico's comment thread. That said, here the sense of a present being destroyed is not the "in between time" of a present in which information is unavailable but rather that of the media itself, through the way the material trace of time on the site (the duration of a thread) is advanced toward its limits. This again raises questions about authorship, in that individual instances of writing or use appear to lose their value as acts of signification but rather contribute to a general sense of excitement produced through the ways users interact with the site's interface.

Looking at an individual case of a happening-turned-thread can help us better understand what this might look like. A thread posted at 6:52 a.m. on September 12, 2005—"You guys, my apartment might be a *matsuri*" (*omaera, ore no apaato ga matsuri kamoshiren*)—was almost instantly overwhelmed with exited posts, reaching its limit of one thousand entries by 8:41 a.m., less than two hours later. The thread began with a post explaining how the apartment of the OP (original poster) had become overrun with what appeared to be maggot larvae emanating from the room next door. The first message—a reply made only sixteen seconds after the thread first appeared on the forum—was a post that read "2." The second reply was similarly not related to the content of the OP, stating "first of all, thanks for posting" (*mazu up*, with the U being written in *hiragana* and the P in roman letters), a common start to a thread. It wasn't until the sixth message in the thread that someone made a direct reference to the subject of the OP, with the poster ironically wondering aloud "I wonder if they'll find the corpses of two children in the closet." The tenth message made a similar joke, writing "it's probably (the remains of) my pet who ran away from home" (*nigeta petto kamishiren ore no*). By the twentieth post to the thread, the "conversation" began to focus, with users responding to one another and with more messages addressing the topic of the thread rather than adding unrelated chatter. This all occurred within three minutes of the original post. The thread continued with more posts joking about the smell of dead bodies and other possible sources of the maggots, even speculating about the landlord of the building, possibly a criminal in hiding.

From this one case we can see some of the characteristics of 2channel and the cultures of online happening that both Suzuki and Hamano touch on. The use of gag-like communication that accumulates energy as more and more posters jump on the same jokes stands out in particular. Qualities of "contentless" communication also appear, especially early on in the thread's life, when what it is about has yet to be settled, not to mention the sense of acceleration of posting as more and more users start to contribute. But to return to the notion of happening as a general phenomenon in anonymous online spaces, this case (both as representative of 2channel and an individual event) has many differences with the kind of experience of time that Hamano perceives in the comment feed on Niconico, which he also describes as a kind of internet *matsuri* or happening.

Due to the recorded nature of videos on the site, these happenings are something that can also be reexperienced over and over. On the one hand, this is different from the kind of events that Suzuki looks at, in that the event of the happening occurs completely in the imaginary space of the site and its interface (*naibu*), whereas the kinds of out-of-control threads that Suzuki writes about tend to refer to something happening outside of the site and involve a sense of "invasion" (*shinkō*) or intrusion.[9] But in regard to the issue of time, this sense of happening that Hamano identifies as being ingrained in Niconico's interface and its surrounding culture of use is one that potentially never ends and can be reexperienced at the whim of the viewer. Hamano's description of 2channel as a culture of *matsuri*, in which threads are rushed to their closing and locking, is in some ways the opposite of this. The sense of finality is foregrounded heavily in how users of the site interact with it through its design elements, and the experience of high energy or excitement one might feel while posting in a thread that is rocketing toward its end cannot be reexperienced once the thread is closed. You instead have to find a new thread and move on, beginning or contributing to a barrage once again.

However, these two cases of online happenings do have some resonance with how Hamano classifies these sensations as something experienced after the fact. In other words, while the videos posted to Niconico were recorded and uploaded in the past, and the comments made by other users were also from a previous experience of watching and writing, we experience them as a kind of "live" or present experience of time through the qualities of pseudo-synchronicity that the site engenders. This sense of liveness is thus something produced from a composite of previous experiences and rendered as a present after those accumulated experiences have all ended and vanished into history. This representation of time might remind us of Henri Bergson's notion of a "thick" present that carries the past with it through the experience of duration and memory (Bergson 1990, 152). There is, in other words, a synthesis of different instances of time that are experienced as an expansion of the present—a thickening—that carries new weight and meaning but is also beyond reach. We will return to this notion of "thickness" shortly in relation to practices of accumulation and transmission.

The quality of being able to reexperience a Niconico video on should also be examined in greater detail. Because the design of the site will roll over older comments in favor of newly entered ones once that feed's limit of one thousand messages has been reached, the message-content of a video can change radically from viewing to viewing. This, of course, isn't as pronounced an issue for videos that have low comment entry counts, in which nothing will be erased as newer comments appear until that limit is reached. But in the case of very popular videos or videos that have been available for many years, the comment feed from one viewing could be completely different from the next. The example of the comment artist's posts in the dancing video of "Sweet Magic" mentioned in chapter 2 is one such example of this. The comment art that traces the movement of the arms and hands of the dancer in the video were entered within a few days of the video being uploaded to the site. But as more responses were entered into the feed (many of which were expressing excitement or admiration in seeing the original comment art), the colorful patterns and designs of the comment art were removed from the video's active feed in favor of newer messages. As such, viewers who may have watched the video early on in its life and, having remembered seeing the impressive designs made in the comment feed, would likely be disappointed to discover that those images had disappeared upon returning to the video at a later date. Similarly, users who arrived too late to witness the earlier version of the video's comment feed may have lost their chance to ever see that particular comment art. This sense of vanishing is amplified by the existence of remainder comments that refer to the missing comment art, such as praise for the comment artist and exclamations of surprise, which now refer to an absent piece.

## Rewriting, Again and Again

Looking at different instances of the comment feed from the same video can help clarify what kind of transformations might occur and how the notion of the video plus comment feed as an object of media is inherently unstable.[10] One example can be found in the Niconico comment feed for "Struck even two times . . ." (*ni do mo butta knows . . .*). First posted on September 4, 2010, this video is a mashup of footage from the classic television anime *Mobile Suit Gundam* (1977) with music from the anime song "God Knows" by Hirano Aya. As of March 19, 2020, the video had received 2,231,654 views and generated 24,943 comments. Many of the most common and popular styles of commenting appear throughout the messages in comment feed's history, such as the deliberate "mishearing" lyrics (*soramimi*) to produce comedic effects, transcription of lyrics and dialogue written as subtitles, and barrages of colorful patterns and shapes posted in swarms of repeating blocks of text. However, because of the video's incredible popularity, even these well-received comments do not last very long due to the way that new comments are continuously being made and pushing out the older messages as they are entered. There is a continual process of erasure and reinscribing.

Observing some of the comments that appeared with the video at different points during its history on Niconico can demonstrate this. For example, on August 17, 2013, the comment feed featured subtitles literally transcribing the dialogue spoken by the characters in the video. However, in the feed on May 30, 2011, subtitles instead engaged in deliberate mishearing, repeating the joke of mishearing the word *kisama* (an aggressive, masculine way of saying "you" spoken by one of the characters) as "Kiss Summer" (see fig. 3.1). The feed from December 3, 2011, featured comment art counting the number of times Captain Bright strikes Amuro, which, given the video's quick editing and repetition of looped footage, was rendered in a swarm of comments flying across the screen and stacked in a column to represent the chaos of the scene (Figure 3.2). As such, at different moments in the video's history the comment feed can take on different personalities, with widely divergent sources of humor or comment art favored from one instance to the next. In some cases this can be attributed to the efforts of a single user who commits to a particular type of writing but in others

**FIGURE 3.1.** Comments in the Niconicofeed from May 30, 2011, react to images from an edited animation using mishearing (*soramimi*), with the word *kisama* ("you," or "you wretch") rendered as "Kiss Summer." Another user comments, "You know, 'Kiss Summer' is kind of old, lololol."

**FIGURE 3.2.** In this Niconico comment art of December 3, 2011, scrolling text and a column of text count the number of times Captain Bright hits Amuro.

a bandwagon in which a joke or style of writing is picked up by many users and repeated ad nauseam.

It isn't just the continous cycle of new comments and "rolling over" of the feed that changes how a video like this might appear at any given moment. Users of the site will also sometimes appropriate a video for a particular event or occasion, transforming the comment feed into a thematized expression of an idea or sentiment. For example, if we look at the history of the comment feed for the video *Starrysky IKZOLOGIC Remix* (previously discussed in relation to mishearing in chapter 2) we can see how a single video might be temporarily claimed a certain cause or event. This video is a mash-up of previously existing music videos that was first uploaded to Niconico on April 26, 2008. It remixes the sound and image tracks from a variety of sources, drawing on the music video and television performance appearances of Yoshi Ikuzo's famous song "I'll Go to Tokyo" (*Ora Tōkyō sa igu da*), which had become a widely used in-joke on Niconico starting in early 2008, as well as the music video for "Starry Sky" by Capsule and similar promotional videos for "Technologic" by Daft Punk and "Ch-Check It Out" by the Beastie Boys. Throughout different points in its history on the site, the comment feed of this video has been taken over for different purposes. When Adam Yauch of the Beastie Boys died in May 2012, the comment feed was filled with messages expressing affection for him and his music, with some simply "RIP MCA" (MCA being Yauch's handle in the group) and others commenting on how young he was at the time of his death or wishing him a peaceful journey into the next life (*yasuraka ni*).

More extreme than this was when, in the wake of the March 11, 2011, earthquake, tsunami, and nuclear disaster, the video was appropriated as a "message video" to express support for those affected. Featuring the tag "Support Song for Victims of the Disaster" (*namisaimono ōen songu*) and a message about trying to make people smile in a time of hardship, the comment feed was temporarily taken over by well-wishing users. This version of the comment feed concluded with over a minute of messages of users posting where they were sending their support from. This moved away from the normally ironic and entertainment-oriented stance of comments in favor of something more sincere, but it also shifted the sense of community on the site away from its local practices of humor and anonymity (by disclosing personal infromation such as location) to express solidarity with all Japan as a nation-state by centering experience around a single event.

## The Problem of the Present

These cases also raise more general questions about performing research on evanescent media such as the comment feed on Niconico or threads posted to 2channel. What is the object of study with media forms that seem to constantly shift and transform? Film and media studies typically approach media texts as discrete objects (even when analyzed in a discursive field), but issues of practice and transformation must also be attended to. The matter of whether these media constitute an archive—and what type of archive—also lingers. To begin to answer the first question, so far this book has been concerned more with the types of writing that appear in the comment feed of various videos than it has with the content of the videos themselves or the particular modes of performance that users of a site take up and display in the videos they make. This focus will shift in chapters 4 and 5, which will analyze "let's play" videos of recorded play of computer and video games. For the present, thinking about the comment feed as a semi-distinct site of focus, it might be necessary to shift from looking for a discrete, identifiable, permanent object and return to some of the concepts introduced earlier on in this chapter. Diana Taylor's work on repertoire as an alternative for thinking about archives and acts of transmission can help address the second question: "What kind of an archive are these media?"

Taylor, in resisting the power of the archive, describes writing as a kind of erasure that, in the act of "legitimizing" an event through the act of recording, also performs a kind of destructive task by transforming one act or event into something else by interpreting it in a particular way (Taylor 2003, 41). For Taylor, this is tied to larger issues of the loss of agency through the authorization of the perspective of the colonizer (such as rendering dispossession as consent in acts of colonization). For the type of media under discussion here, there is another kind of erasure of experience that happens through the way that the sites record and store text. It is particularly through a logic of accumulation that the comment feed of Niconico and the thread system of 2channel might push us toward thinking of them not as discrete, discernible media objects or events but instead a kind of aesthetic culture and ongoing process. In this aesthetic, acts of writing engage not in content-based communication but are rather a kind of noise or, as Hamano writes, "excitement" (*nori*). Affective modes of writing take priority over literalness. We will return to the notion of accumulation in regard to summary (*matome*) sites and video-sharing sites as a kind of storage in the next chapter. For now, the focus will be on thinking about these media not as static objects or events but rather as mediating processes that are always rewriting and updating themselves through the architecture of use and participation that is inscribed in their makeup.

The quality of accumulation is not necessarily one of storage or saving. "Entropy" might be a more accurate word to describe the type of accumulation of writing that these sites engender. They instill a mode of participation that is seemingly concerned less with communication than in riding a kind of wave of excitement or sense of momentum. Disintegration of archives is, of course, relevant to other and assumedly more permanent types of writing, such as bound volumes in libraries, scrolls, and manuscript pages.[11] However, in the case of online writing, the disintegration of the archive is not necessarily something that is unintentional and unavoidable due to the powers of nature and material existence but rather something that is programmed into the very design of sites' interfaces.

This can be taken as a sign of the economy of participation that is commonly described in writing on the internet and social media. By making individual instances of participation in the media impermanent, the makers and operators of sites have created incentive for their audience to return to the site and participate over and over, thus producing more opportunities to draw on their labor for generating revenue. However, returning to the question of entropy as a kind of aesthetic quality of these sites, there is also a type of forgetting that these sites initiate through the rollover of the comment feed and locking and discarding of threads. The impermanence of the individual instances of use on the site is foregrounded in the very act of use, suggesting disempowerment of individual acts or events in creating meaning. The horizon of participation is shifted to a more general, abstract culture of the site that emerges through these patterns of use. In other words, what is salient in producing the culture of these sites is not the complete picture of many individual, connected moments of participation or use but rather the process of continuously writing and rewriting that emerges out of this environment of impermanence and excitement.[12]

This sense of accumulation brings us back to Bergson's notion of a "thick" present. Bergson's writings on duration and time have been used in cinema studies to describe the effects of projection and ordering of images in sequence, and we might borrow from that concept to think about how the fluxional succession of writing events on 2channel and in the comment feed of Niconico points to a related kind of effect. The relationship between memory and anticipation that Bergson describes as filling this "thickness" seems particularly relevant when considering the way the automated locking of threads on 2channel suggests a certain form of writing and the automated rolling over of comments on Niconico creates an ongoing sense of erasure and rewriting. The sense of time that these media suggest in their architectures is one that is in flux, constantly refiguring the relationship between the present form of a thread or comment feed and its previous and future iterations. They are never finished but instead always being augmented and moving into new stages of transformation. The "thickness" of these media is thus something born out of their logic of (re)writing and overwriting.

Following this train of thought, we should pause to consider the significance of the present as a distinct state of time and experience. The idea of the present intersects with acts of forgetting in other kinds of media, and media scholars such as Terje Rasmussen have noted the significance of forgetting in producing a sense of legibility in time, from which an experience and recognition of the present can emerge (Rasmussen 2010, 112). In many other types of media this means equating acts of selection, editing, overlooking, and recording what appears significant with forgetting other events or experiences of time, but in the case of automated forgetting, as in Niconico and 2channel, we might consider a different kind of relationship between forgetting and the present. Hamano's concepts of pseudo-synchronicity on Niconico and selective synchronicity on Twitter suggest two ways of thinking about how the present *feels* like a present, but, keeping in mind the orientation toward time that these sites engender, we should also think about what kind of present they might suggest.

## Aesthetics of Rehearsal

Thus far this chapter has described the aesthetics of writing on 2channel and Niconico in terms of accumulation of text, acceleration of activity, and foregrounding of the experience of time through the anticipation of an end or closing. This has elaborated on the concept of textual cacophony to complement the discussion in chapters 1–2. Accumulation is not, however, only experienced in terms of erasure, overwriting, and loss. The constant production of text that the users of these sites engage with also initiates cultures of writing that, as described in chapter 1, can foreground the pictorial or image-oriented properties of text as much as linguistic or denotational content. While the writing over an image or over other comments might be considered destructive in some sense, the distinct kinds of writing that appear out of these practices also suggest creativity. However, as already noted, it is not only cultures of writing that this kind of animated text production entails but also cultures of reading that recognize, interpret, and reproduce it. This section will look at rehearsals of local writing and reading practices in greater detail, focusing on the reproduction of text through practices such as copypasta writing—the use of formatted blocks of text—and the rehearsal of content from previous comment feeds.

Let's look at one famous example from 2channel. On January 22, 2000, a user posted a thread with the title "I Laughed at the Great Hanshin Earthquake!" As the title suggests, this thread is in many ways emblematic of the popular perception of 2channel as a hive of antagonistic and politically vicious communities gathering to mock the general public. The post begins by repeating the thread title, then asking: "I am the only one who counted the thousands of dead bodies, one by one?" The post continues with this crude tone, with the user claiming to have clapped as he watched the news unfold on TV and ultimately been disappointed that only some six thousand people had died as a result of the disaster. More and more outrageous claims follow, such as the poster's contempt for those who perished or were made distraught by the disaster and his declaration of traveling to Kobe (one of the cities hit hardest by the earthquake) to take commemorative photographs. More gallows humor is expressed through sarcastic frustration at the tax money that will be used to pay for the cleanup and rebuilding of the region's infrastructure. For many, this kind of cynical humor that elicits outrage from the reader is characteristic of 2channel's distinct brand.

Suzuki Kensuke uses this thread as one of his examples for writing about the culture of online happenings on 2channel. He notes the way that the thread was reproduced with altered text after the terrorist attacks in New York City on September 11, 2001, with the content changed to address the new event, such as the counting of dead bodies becoming counting falling buildings and towers (Suzuki, 37). He also points to English translations of the post that were produced with online, automated translation software and then posted to sites such as Yahoo. In all cases the structure and tone of the post is almost identical, with the only changes being in the details of its content, such as the names of individual places and references to local news coverage. The general structure and tone was consistent in the different versions, with a cynical tone and self-presentation of emotional detachment. Whitney Phillips has noted how these types of "disaster joke" threads and postings have become a common part of online troll culture in the contemporary age of sensationalistic media coverage of disasters and images of public (and private) trauma.[13]

The "I Laughed" thread was also reproduced in its entirety and without alteration on multiple occasions, such as February 22, 2000, and March 3, 2001, although in the short amount of time between postings the thread had already become famous enough to be recognized by many readers. Other posts in these repeated threads referred to the use of rewritten, formatted blocks of text, noting "this is a famous gag" (*meineta*) or referring to the post as a parody or mimicry of the perceived original (*motoneta*). Over the years since "I Laughed" was written and posted, the thread has become known as a significant part of 2channel's history and been documented on many summary sites and wikis. Following the triple disaster of March 11, 2011, the thread was reproduced again, now taking on the title "I Laughed at the Great Kanto Earthquake!" In this version the post responded to another major earthquake-related catastrophe, so the content was practically unchanged. However, this time the laughter focused on Tokyo rather than Kansai, a noteworthy reversal given that part of the sneering tone of the original post was due to its projection of Tokyo snobbery over other regions of Japan.

The content of these types of posts is, of course, highly offensive to many readers, and in many ways that is part of the point for the communities that first produced and enjoyed these threads. It is, as with many of the other types of comments discussed in chapters 1 and 2, based in a kind of spectacle. As with the example of anti-Korean protests in Odaiba from the introduction, the grounding of actual-world events and prejudices in the cultural and aesthetic sphere of anonymous communication forms the ambivalent, ironic mode that fuels this of spectacularization of social and cultural angst. These examples similarly document the political tendencies of anonymous media cultures to return to those same networks of meaning and structures of identification despite fantasies of being unmarked or unburdened by actual-world systems of association.

The use of copypasta blocks of text and ASCII art is one of the most pronounced features of 2channel's community and its modes of writing, and the above example ("I Laugh") presents a case where the culture and memory of the site is transmitted and perpetuated through repetition of famous events in the site's history. This quality of self-documentation and its intersection with elitism and ironic laughter can also be considered part of the transference of identification away from the individual and toward the site and its associated cultural practices. Hamano has claimed that users "become" the character of 2channel by participating in the characteristic culture of the site through things like ironic humor, nationalistic discourse, and the management of membership through "in jokes" (Hamano 2008a, 95, 112). Following this notion of cultures of online anonymity as continuously rehearsing the same (or similar) practices, we can return to Diane Taylor's suggestion of performance as an alternative to conventional archives and characterize these modes of writing as a kind of culture of transmission and repertoire. Indeed, one of my major goals in this book is to characterize anonymity through the intersections between its social and aesthetic practices.

Looking at comment feeds on Niconico that continuously reproduce similar messages offers another case for thinking about how the cultures of these sites might posit individual language events not as discrete acts of writing with their own sense of authorship but rather as chains of circulation and a distributed sense of repeated (non)authorship. The feed for the video *Blood Clan Temple: Free Your Passions—"Let's Go! Omyoji"* is one such example. Originally posted on March 6, 2007, it is known as the "oldest video" (*saiko no dōga*) on the site in its tags and has generated over fifteen million views and more than four million comments as of June 23, 2016. Its images are taken from a promotional video attached to a PlayStation 2 fighting game. The strangeness of the chanting and dancing characters from a period-setting fighting game has captured the attention of users of the site since it was first uploaded. As with previous examples, many of the repeated jokes in the comment feed are based on deliberate mishearing (*soramimi*) that makes fun of the dialogue spoken by the characters, posted as subtitles that coincide with the dialogue. This also includes self-deprecating references to the users of the site, using language like "NEET," which stands for "No education, employment, or training" and has become a common expression and label in post-recession Japan (fig. 3.3). Other repeated instances include fake credits posted during a guitar solo in the middle of the song, with each iteration having a different name or credit. But more generally it is the quality of *danmaku*—overwhelming tides of comments that almost block out the screen in a barrage—that has been repeated over and over throughout the video's history, constantly reappearing as older comments become phased out. For example, the chanting of "Disperse the Evil Spirits!" (*akuryō taisan*) is always accompanied by bold, colorful blocks of text that rush past the screen.

Similar cases can be found on other videos in which chanting or hooks in songs have been taken up for mass-commenting, such as the refrain of "okkusenman!" in videos using the background music from a Dr. Wily stage in the Megaman 2 video game (originally released as Rockman 2 in Japan). As with other comment feeds, these moments of seemingly endless repetition are both creative and destructive in that they push older comments out of the feed while often re-creating content found in those older comments. What emerges, then, is a

**FIGURE 3.3.** Comments in Japanese are projected over a Blood Clan video from March 25, 2009, on Niconico, along with "NEET," which stands for "No education, employment, or training."

chain of repetition in which familiar patterns or jokes are restaged over and over, in some ways new through their reintroduction into the comment feed (and sometimes with different color text or font size) but also stuck in a seemingly never-ending cycle of repetition and re-creation in their subordination to what has become recognized as the normalized comment feed for a particular video.

This type of restaging similar comments over and over might remind of us Judith Butler's observations about repetition in her model of performances of gender. Butler notes that "performativity is not a single act" and that even the "act" itself is not a discrete unit of time or language or gesture but rather part of a more general chain of "sedimentation" that gains "act-like status" through this continuous process of accumulation and reference to the past.[14] In the case of comment feeds on Niconico, we might actually be able to locate an original from which subsequent feeds develop and that they refer to, but there is also a related quality of circulation that, as with the preclusion of individual authorship, suggests a transfer of reference away from an isolatable moment in a video's history to a more abstract sense of the identity that the video's comment feed itself has accumulated over time. The experience of time suggested by these practices would also seem to move away from one of history (which we might think of as a linear progression or sequencing of events) to one of the archive (an accumulation of a feeling of the past and of cultural memory tied to the media object in question).

But what is also provocative about Butler's notion of repetition and performance here is the quality of mimesis that tries to re-create what is (mis)perceived as an ideal model of being. This performance of re-creation is always imperfect, failing to reproduce exactly what is held up as the ideal model of imitation. This repeated failure is, however, also creative in that categories of identity such as man and woman emerge out of this field of repeated performances. In other words, this kind of mimetic performance is not just an attempt at materially reproducing a preexisting category. Rather, the very category is generated out of the circulation of failed performances and the chain of discourse that emerges around them.

The repetition of things like *danmaku* comment barrage and modular variations of popular jokes can be considered from a related perspective. The attempt to continuously reproduce what is perceived as a series of comments characterizing or belonging to a particular video and its feed is not only an act that engenders that sense of affixing meaning to a specific video page. It is also the sense of identification built on a continuous chain of small differences that are constantly renegotiating similarity and variation with other versions of the same feed. The sedimentation of a distinct style of commenting with a video is thus also something that emerges out of a sense of time that might be experienced as the present. We perceive what "belongs" through observing multiple acts of repeated commenting, suggesting a sense of retrospective or recollected identification between ways of writing in a particular video feed.

However, as Butler notes, this kind of repetition also "implies that every act is itself a recitation, the citing of a prior chain of acts which are implied in a present act and which perpetually drain any 'present' act of its presentness."[15] In that sense, a chain of repeated textual performance that congeals around a specific set of writing might suggest a sense of the "present" by locating a single moment in that larger, more general series of repeated performances. But the meaning of any single "present" also becomes "drained" of any specific meaning through its near interchangeability with any other moment of time in the same chain of repeated comment feeds. Thus, as with the emergence of a sense of the present through anticipation in the culture of happening on 2channel, the emergence of a sense of the present in the comment feed for popular videos on Niconico (those with many thousands or even millions of comments) is one of accumulation and sedimentation of the archival past.

This notion of continuous citation of the past is also a key element in what Sasaki Toshinao describes as "curation" (Sasaki 2011). This entails relating a present thing or act to what has come before it and producing a value system based on an archive of materials that produces context and familiarity. This continual reference to the past in order to animate the present involves a process of sedimentation similar to what Butler has described in relation to gender performance. Curation is thus best understood as a kind of interstitial activity that happens not only between individuals (the curator and the consumer or audience in Sasaki's model) but also between different registers of time. However, curation as a distinct act is perhaps not readily visible in practices such as repeating or simulating previous comments on Niconico, as the lack of attribution makes it impossible to measure how many individuals are performing this sense of repetition. The labor of curation is thus something that, as with the practices this chapter been describing, is distributed across the user base of these sites and not something that any one individual owns or holds authorship over. It becomes a kind of network sociality and network aesthetic but also something that reflecting atomized social existence and the desire for new forms of human (dis)connection that accompany that way of living.

The next chapter will extend this analysis of how time, repetition, and disjunction figure in online media culture. The focus will shift to questions of labor, copyright, and loss, using summary (*matome*) sites and video-sharing portals as case studies. We will also consider how these demonstrate barrage-style media's engagement with popular culture via a logic of consumption, along with the diminished status of authorship and originality in online media texts and content.

# 4
# COLLECTING, COPYING, AND COPYRIGHT

The automated deletion of user-generated content provides one way to frame the study of user participation in online media. The preceding chapter discussed how users of 2channel and Niconico post the same material over and over, replacing old content almost as soon as it was deleted. A perhaps more common example of this type of deletion of media content in online platforms is when media is removed due to copyright violations or claims. Commercially produced and released movies, music, and television are often shared by users on sites such as YouTube and Dailymotion, only to be taken down following a complaint or copyright strike by the copyright holder. These too, however, are often quickly reposted or shared once more, leading to another chain deletion and reposting as media industries battle would-be file sharers.

That said, not only commercial media content is subject to this pattern. User-generated content from blogs and social media have also frequently been collected, edited, and reappropriated through summary portals, often without proper attribution to their original creators. This is a consequence of the default anonymity settings in some cases. Such aggregation portals are known as *matome* (summary) sites in Japan, and throughout the 2000s and early 2010s they grew into a popular supplement (or even substitute) for consuming online media due to their ability to highlight the most important or amusing parts of a thread or exchange. They offer a digest form of social media consumption, providing something of a break from the overflowing, runaway pace of cacophonous media. However, as with the sharing of commercially produced video content, this also represents a repackaging of material by another party, one who is neither the author nor the owner of said content. The resonance between this type of media use and file-sharing extends to the networks of labor that have developed around collecting this material for distribution, including how the venues for sharing are maintained by a passionate user base. As such, while qualities of authorship appear to recede in these types of impermanent media, user labor continues to grow and change to keep up with new challenges.

This chapter will continue the discussion on impermanence in online media by turning from accumulation and rewriting in a single media form (such as the comment feed of a video) and instead at practices of collecting, editing, and curating across distinct media services. The adaptation of content across media platforms will be important to consider, as will the agency of collecting and reworking those materials. The first point of focus for this discussion will be summary sites, a type of blog that summarizes the contents of popular threads from 2channel and presents them in abridged form. This can offer a bridge to previous topics within the theme of accumulation of textual writing. But, in keeping with one of the subthemes of this book (the intersections between television and online media), we will also examine video-sharing sites that have come to provide alternative access to television content and the cultures of sharing that have appeared around these a sites.[1] This brings the present analysis in closer in alignment with discussions of media convergence in Japan but also reframes aspects of online media culture as issues of adaptation.[2]

## Collection and Curation

Summary (*matome*) sites have been a significant presence in online media in Japan almost as long as the platforms they draw their content from. Furthermore, these sites come in all shapes and sizes, running the gambit from amateur and fan-run ventures to commercial sites with fully integrated advertising and promotion systems. Our focus here will be on sites that adapted the content produced in threads on 2channel (before the site rebranded as 5channel in October 2017). The general concept behind these sites is to collect and offer digest versions of the content from popular threads posted to mother sites. They resemble news aggregation sites in their purpose and presentation but often focus on user-produced content from social media rather than commercial content written by journalists or professional bloggers. As with many other web forums with heavy user traffic, 2channel produced an overwhelming amount of new threads and reply posts every day, hour, and minute. The sheer volume of topics and subtopics that appeared on the site could be daunting for users, and it would be an enormous (if not impossible) challenge for anyone to keep up with the constant barrage of new content.[3]

One reason summary sites became so popular was their ability to help navigate the vast amount of content produced on 2channel, offering users a digest version to peruse.[4] Most summary sites are hosted on blog pages, such as FC2 (*Himasoku* is a well-known example) and Livedoor (such as *Itai nyuusu*). The most popular of these survived 2channel's closure, often by shifting their focus to collecting content from Twitter and other social media platforms. Some of these sites also have a specialized focus, such as collecting stories about a particular type of media or an individual performer or musical act. These then become part of the distribution of information for audiences and fans, who can more easily keep on top of developments regarding their favorite anime, band, or comedian. General purpose *matome* sites can also help users to wade through the mountain of material to find the hidden gems and highlights of each days' worth of new posts and topics.

Not every thread posted to 2channel would be or could have been copied and saved to a summary site, and those that were saved did not typically survive in complete form. Abridged versions of threads typically contain the most humorous or interesting posts or those that generated the greatest reaction but often cut out the posts that simply read "lol" or the like. In comparison to the general sense of excitement and "killing time" that we might find in the original threads, the tone on summary sites is decidedly more content-focused and with less filler or chatter between the messages that communicate something specific.

The summary site Painful News (*Itai nyuusu*) posted a summary of the thread "'Go die' is being used instead of greetings?! Actual state of the Judo world" on March 13, 2013, the same day the original thread had been posted to 2channel. The summary version of the thread included the opening post and added an image that had not been part of the message posted to 2channel, which does not host images. Furthermore, of the first twenty-five replies to the thread, only seven were carried over to the summary version. The posts that were saved for the summarized version all refer to the use of the verb "to die" (*shine*) on 2channel, highlighting the gag that runs throughout the thread and what likely inspired the story to be posted to the site in the first place. The user posting the third message in the thread jokes "that's common-sense level on 2chan" (*2chan de ha jōshiki reberu*), while the sixth message reads "It's as if it's you guys, lol" (*marude omaera jyan w*). The twenty-third reply makes a sophisticated meta-knowledge joke about the site, *shine nara seefu*, in which *shine* is written with one of the common orthographic substitutions that replaces the character for "to die" (死ね) with the one for marking family names or formal titles (氏ね). Further replies staged imaginary conversations that include "go die" as a cheerful greeting between friends or coworkers.

In total, forty-eight posts were carried over from the hundreds of replies made to the original post. The general sense one has in comparing the summarized version with the original is of continuity—almost all of the posts that have been saved and reposted are ones that take up the joke of how "go die" is used on 2channel, with all of the other chatter and responses removed to make the summarized thread read as a more coherent conversation that flows from one response to the next.

The issue of digital labor lurks behind the practices of curation and reading that go into producing summary sites. On the one hand, these sites obviously generate revenue for their hosts and administrators through advertising directed at their readers, which in a way transforms the act of browsing the site into a kind of labor to be appropriated. But they also partially free their audience from the labor of reading. 2channel is, in terms of browsing, overwhelming for individual users due to the sheer volume of content present from one subforum to the next and from thread to thread. This is compounded by the amount of visual information that can be displayed in a single screen and the use of opaque forms of writing and related practices that refuse immediate comprehension. Summary sites might not do much about the latter. Indeed, some add color and different font sizes to text in a way that emphasizes their pictorial nature. Many also fill their screens with ads (animated and static), images of manga, anime, glamour idols, banners, and link-heavy sidebars, often to the point that an alternate aesthetic of clutter and distraction emerges.[5]

Along with this shift in the labor of reading is a pivot from the kind of happening or *matsuri*-like experience of time. The anticipation of the end of a thread on 2channel is replaced by a sense of archival time that renders text as always already part of the past and unavailable for the kind of meta-interaction or sense of participation that a live thread might contains. Many summary sites will include a subsection in which users can comment on the saved thread and messages transferred from 2channel, but these become part of a distinct sequence of commentary that does not engage with the same possibilities of "killing time" or experiencing acceleration and accumulation of writing. The shift in the experience (and performance) of time is echoed by the shift from ending and toward something like storage. The method of storage and curation found on these summary sites is, by nature of their tendency to edit, remove, and transform content from 2channel threads, also about loss and deletion. As such, although the general principle of saving content from an ephemeral type of media like a 2channel thread might at first glance set these sites apart from media discussed previously, there remains a connection through the continuous sense of loss and of remainder that occurs through the way the sites are operated.

In addition to the politics of digital labor present in the practice of curation of these sites, the relationship between summary sites and 2channel has not always been a friendly one. Summary sites perhaps helped to widen 2channel's audience and even sustain interest in the site by offering digest versions of its content, but they also attract attention away from the original site and eat away at its ability to generate revenue through advertising and views.[6] The appropriation of user made content from threads on 2channel and use of that material in commercial ventures has also been viewed with suspicion by ordinary users of the site. Should, for example, users have control over—or even rights to—content they post, even if it is unattributed? 2channel's ability to control or influence the administrators of summary sites has also not always been clear, even when dealing with the question of copyright or intellectual property rights.

Those questions come to the forefront of the summary-producing community in June 2012 when 2channel's creator and owner Nishimura Hiroyuki (typically referred to as Hiroyuki in both 2channel and Niconico) announced that he would be prohibiting use of material from 2channel on five popular summary sites.[7] Many summary sites had previously had an uneasy relationship with 2channel's administrators, but this was one of the most direct and severe prohibitions seen up to that point. Some *matome* sites were forced to transform in response to this new prohibition against copying content from the main site, while others merely scaled back the amount of 2channel-derived content they would publish.[8] 2channel's frustration over the use of its content on summary sites also resonates with some of the themes of individual authorship disappearing into distributed networks and aggregate social forms that have been discussed throughout this book.

Issues of ownership of the site and its content were thrown into greater chaos between 2014 and 2017. After years of financial and legal contention Hiroyuki was forced out of his role on 2channel when the site was acquired by N.T. Technologies (an American company) in early 2014, which led to a power struggle between Hiroyuki and the new owners. Not happy to give up his prized creation, Hiroyuki developed an alternative to 2channel (2ch.net), 2ch.sc.[9] This was essentially a real-time mirror of the site maintained by a spider program bot that would browse and index the original (2ch.net) on the new 2ch.sc.[10] This is in some ways comparable to a DDoS attack (distributed denial of service) and caused the original site to go down on several occasions. When confronted by frustrated users of 2channel about their problems accessing the site, Hiroyuki explained his actions by claiming that he was backing up the content that he, as founder of 2channel, holds copyright over.[11]

Struggles with control over *matome* sites vexed the new American owners at N.T. just as they had Hiroyuki. Indeed, similar problems began to emerge for English-language sites such as reddit and 4chan, who also saw their content being harvested by digest portals.[12] Plans to limit third-party access to

2channel comments went unfulfilled, and by 2017 the site had been sold to yet another owner. In order to avoid lingering struggles over copyright, the site was rebranded as 5channel and its domain changed to 5ch.net. 2channel's sale to an American company was met by an ironic symmetry in 2015 when 4chan, the English-language derivative of 2channel and its image-board equivalent, *futaba channel*, was sold to Hiroyuki (Isaac 2015).

The drama over 2channel, *matome* sites, and the contested authority over copyright and labor represents many of the transformations of life and work under neoliberalism in the early twenty-first century. The Web 2.0 model of internet media and commerce thrived by turning user-created content and unpaid service (such as moderation and curation roles) into ways of extracting value from the time and energy of these sites' user bases, and this was frequently advanced by having audiences self-select themselves based on interests connected with commercial media and popular culture. The numerous categories and sub-categories for discussion topics on 2channel (displayed in a long list of unadorned hyperlinks) demonstrates how this featured in the most basic site design. *Matome* sites put that sensibility in an additional set of brackets by transforming an existing case of user-driven content and re-presenting it as a digest, furthering the extraction of value from this type of leisure-work activity and the style of internet user it promotes.

Also key to this example is how time is transformed (or made to feel transformed) by way of the asynchronous dimensions of online media. In offering an alternative to combing through an ocean of content on 2channel and presenting the most engaging and satisfying pieces to their user base, *matome* sites provide not only a more easily consumable version of comment threads but also present that content in a way that resonates with the pressures of contemporary work and schooling, in which an individual's time and attention is often stretched thin by competing responsibilities or pursuits. Observing the cluttered, ad-laden design of *matome* sites alongside their premise of curated content, we might then arrive at the conclusion that this type of portal is not necessarily providing relief or escape from that condition of compressed time and social and professional fatigue but rather providing a way of making that condition feel more comfortable or manageable. The postscript of this book will discuss the relationship between fatigue and asynchronous media in greater depth.

## Repackaging Video

As described at the opening of this chapter, collection and curation of online media content is not limited to user-generated content. As around the world, commercial television in Japan has recently begun shifting to internet-based streaming. This can be observed through the localization of commercial services such as Netflix and Amazon Prime, which since 2016 have produced their own content for the Japanese market. And while commercial media production has recently developed into a strong presence in online video in Japan, for the majority of the 2000s and early 2010s a good deal of online video sharing in Japan was done noncommercially via user-based file sharing. Furthermore, many of the platforms used for file sharing by Japanese consumers were actually based in other parts of the world.

One result of this type of file sharing was that video-sharing sites took up a role as a kind of substitute form of television that was able deliver the same kinds of content through a presumably more convenient formant. However, the severity of copyright laws and enforcement of such claims on commercial websites such as YouTube and FC2 often means that any such content uploaded will soon have copyright infringement claims filed against the uploader. These resulting in videos being deleted and, in some cases, the account that uploaded it being suspended. Japan has relatively strict copyright laws in this regard, and domestic media companies are often very aggressive in maintaining control over their properties. The anticipation of a video being deleted after a copyright claim has in turn encouraged patterns of viewing based around expectation of ephemerality. This includes blogs that provide links to video files and regular updates alerting users to newly available content, facilitating a kind of viewing that has become tailored to an environment organized around a sense of acceleration and deletion. Similarly, some users create alternate channels that can host uploaded videos of commercial television that are shared through links on the main channel (often called *honkan*), thus offering a limited form of protection from aggressive copyright claims. Other channels will only make videos publicly viewable for a small period of time each day, with hours posted in the channel profile or video description so viewers can plan in advance to watch something before it is made temporarily unavailable again. This leads to a culture of maintenance as users will re-upload the same videos or try to find ways to prevent their videos from being deleted.[13]

The irony of this situation is that the fantasy of on-demand viewing of television through the internet—that of allowing the viewer to watch a show whenever he or she chooses or at his or her own leisure—has found itself bound to another type of limitation of time, although now based not on the time of broadcast but rather on the immediacy of the threat of copyright and deletion. A side effect of this wide-reaching apparatus of copyright avoidance is intensification of an emerging notion of the present—the window of time in which videos are available.[14]

## Transnational Video Networks

As with the user network for collecting and curating material from around the web found on *matome* sites, there exists a growing apparatus of blogs, fan sites, and social media accounts to facilitate the watching of Japanese television online. These sites host and link to all manner of TV content, including weekly dramas, variety, comedy, music shows, and special programming that does not have a regular broadcasting schedule. Links to video-sharing sites are collected and organized on specialty blogs and portal sites, allowing users to easily navigate the seemingly endless sea of uploaded video content. Much of this content is improperly labeled to avoid detection or, more commonly, only available on a non-Japanese-language video site, such as YouTube, Youku, FC2, Kissasia, Bilibili, or Dailymotion. Such an approach adds the additional complexity of translation and difficulty of use into the mix, despite the original impulse to use online hosting to provide easier access and a greater flexibility of time than what broadcast formats allow for. The assumed shift in how people now watch television programs (on computers, tablets, or phones instead of TV sets) is thus also increasingly buttressed by a shift in the cultures of watching that develop around these alternative ways of saving, distributing, and commenting on television content.

Following developments similar to how 2channel summary *matome* sites are organized and maintained, the energy and labor of finding, cataloging, and storing these videos has become distributed across a growing community of users who help initiate a different kind of labor of watching. This change in spectatorship has had an impact on how television is produced and distributed, and the shift from conventional forms of watching has aggravated the sense of dropping ratings for television in Japan since the 2000s.[15]

The distinction between categories of use or access such as piracy, appropriation, and fair use frequently disappear with this style of consumption, which often affords convenience of use and access as the strongest priority for the individual. That attitude toward media consumption, which might sacrifice quality of experience in favor of what is the most immediately satisfying, speaks to another aspect of media culture in late-capitalist societies. With those considerations in mind, the remainder of this chapter will look to the communities and cultures of viewing that appear around these constraints and examine what those practices show us about how online media and commercial television are often entwined in cycles of copying from one another.

In the face of copyright challenges, operators of video-sharing sites have developed strategies such as making videos private for most of the day so that they won't be discovered easily, making alterations to the soundtrack or editing the video in such a way so as to be able to claim it as a distinct from the original and therefore not subject to copyright claims, and making multiple accounts to repeatedly upload a video file after it has been deleted elsewhere. YouTube receives the most intense traffic of any online video-sharing site, and its affiliation with internet giant Google also makes it beholden to commercial regulation and copyright law in a way other sites might not be.

For many years a compelling alternative to YouTube in this regard was Youku. Youku is a China-based video-sharing site that appeared in the wake of YouTube's immediate popularity, launching in late 2006, around the same time as Niconico in Japan. As with YouTube, the site has partnerships with many local commercial media companies, who use the site as an alternative way of reaching their audience and broadcasting video content. However, the enforcement of copyright laws on Youku has often been much more relaxed than video sites hosted in the United States, Europe, or Japan face, meaning that many types of commercial video can be uploaded and stored on the site regardless of who owns it. As such, since its creation, the site has become something on an online storage facility for all manner of foreign media, including Japanese television. This has made the site incredibly popular in Japan and for viewers of Japanese television who live elsewhere in the world, who can now enjoy a semi-permanent way of watching shows they may have missed or, perhaps more commonly, an alternative way of watching that does not require a television. There have been many attempts to limit access to the site (as well as Toudu, another China-based video site that has partnered with Youku), but web browser applications that get around the prohibition and use of proxies to allow access have made this difficult.[16] Since 2010, Youku's integration into mainstream commercial media production has caused copyright enforcement to become more strict, which in turn has led audiences of Japanese media to turn to other sites, such as Bilibili. The ability to watch shows "with" other members of the audience via the comment function has also made Bilibili (and related sites such as Mio Mio) more attractive.

The language barrier in using a Chinese-language site might cause a problem for some users, but, as with 2channel summary sites, much of the time and energy one might have to put into browsing has been alleviated by a community of link sharers, video collectors, and site administrators. Blogs on sites such as FC2 collect and organize links to video files on Youku, Bilibili, and elsewhere in easily navigable ways, sorting videos by title and season and even making cast members' names searchable. All a user needs to do is click a link and press "play" on the site's video player. Language is not much of barrier, as the need to be able to read Chinese has been greatly lifted by the development of access-facilitating websites. Much writing on the online culture in China has insisted on a kind of semi-closed, quasi-national status of internet use through elements such as language and censorship, but we should also keep in mind the ways the people use the internet that are not dependent on understanding written language.[17] Similarly, the ways that people around the world use these types of media do not necessarily fall into those types of categorization.

The value of Youku and similar sites is deeply tied to their being based in China and the stance toward copyright that this allows for, but that does not exhaust the way they are used, nor is audience engagement with the sites based purely in geopolitics.[18] We can even consider Youku, Bilibili, and Mio Mio to have become a significant part of the online media environment of Japan due to the type of alternative access they provide for television audiences. This is despite its supposed national and language-specific configuration Users from across the world can log on to these sites to watch all manner of content despite unfamiliarity with written Chinese. The questions to be asked entail time (when we can watch?) and labor and energy (how can we find what we want to watch?) in addition to copyright.

There is also an aesthetics of access in the user interfaces developed around video-sharing on non-Japanese-language sites through blogs that collect links and share them on social media. This includes visual signs such as watermarking in addition to translation elements. Media scholars writing on video recording formats such as VHS have commented on the way access can emerge as an aesthetic property of video media, such as the loss of resolution that comes through duplicating tapes and compression artifacts (distortion) from copying.[19] There is often a visible, almost material inscription that hints at how the media (often bootleg in nature) was circulated. This sort of inscription is not necessarily seen on YouTube and Youku videos, notwithstanding attempts to modify them to avoid copyright. But links to untranslated web pages, notices that a video has been removed, and organization of links and files via portal sites also suggest an aesthetics of access that marks videos' status as bootleg. The typically lower quality of videos shared this way and introduction of watermarks also are a sign of their commercial illegitimacy and the means through which they were made available.

But to return to the questions raised so far in this chapter, what kind of accumulation does a site such as Youku or Bilibili suggest? The method of storage such sites allow for is often attached to a specific sense of time and access, and the very apparatus of access created by their users also transforms the status of these sites in global media culture. We might also ask: "Is Youku an archive?" Similar questions have been raised in regard to YouTube and predecessors like eBaum's World, with some claiming that these sites cannot become an archive due to unreliability in hosting (as videos are taken down), the previously poor quality of the materials it saves, and for engaging in unauthorized hosting and copying (Hilderbrand 2009, 233). For much of its existence, Youku has not faced the same problems of videos being removed due to copyright claim, although there is still no guarantee of continued access due to the everchanging media environment. The same can be said for *danmu* (barrage) sites such as Mio Mio and Bilibili, and as more and more pressure is put on these sites by mainstream institutions, the disappearance of videos will only increase, and, as with previous attempts to limit access to such sites in Japan, logging on or loading a video may also become more difficult.[20]

For users from Japan, most of the value and meaning of these sites comes from their ability to host commercial media content and make it easily accessible. While lax attitudes toward copyright and licensing might normally pose a problem to an institution or organization's status as an archive, in these cases it is that very quality that would seem to grant that type of status. Furthermore, the possibility of Youku and related sites such as Bilibili and Mio Mio becoming online reservoirs of Japanese-language television content is what has led to much online labor—the work of organizing the sharing of videos on these sites. As with sites like 2channel, the quality of accumulation is thus both a blessing and a curse. The availability of so much content requires making it legible and navigable for individual users who do not have the time or energy to sort through seemingly endless material.

There is thus a quality of translation at work in these media of accumulation. I have described above the language (non)barrier posed by the interface of these sites for many non-Chinese-reading users, which can be seen as a kind of translation. But, as with the 2channel summary sites, the transformation of one kind of media content into another is another kind of translation. The production of an alternative interface to allow users to access videos without searching Youku echoes how summary sites provide an alternative way of reading through 2channel in digested form. Indeed, Youku itself offers something of a digest-form of television in Japan by removing the issue of broadcast time and channel programming—you can watch what you want, when you want. Many users will also remove commercials that were included in the original broadcast. This again brings us back to the quality of transformation and flux that infuses so much online media. Similarly, the repetition of comment feed messages on Niconico performs a kind of translation of the feed by distilling a comment feed into what is perceived to be its original or optimal form, accumulated and sedimented over long periods of use and rehearsal. The quality of accumulation salient in these kinds of media, then, is not just one of collecting large volumes of information and content but also entails how that material is transformed into a kind of shared culture or set of cultural practices that are distributed across an audience and user base.

What we are left with are media practices that foreground their nature as always unfinished. Whether evident in discussion threads that are automatically locked and later edited for summary sites, video comment feeds that constantly roll over and repeat similar exchanges, or video storage sites that endlessly dodge copyright claims, the process of transformation and augmentation never ends. As users add or remove content, they perpetuate the cycle of successive iterations that replace one another and add to the growing archive of ambivalence.

## Copying *Danmaku* Aesthetics

So far this chapter has discussed how different types of content have been copied and collected between media platforms. This notion of "copy" can also extend to different types of media aesthetics and interfaces. As previously mentioned, the comment overlay of Niconico has appeared on many sites since its birth in 2006. This is in addition to content from Niconico finding its way onto other video-hosting platforms. To conclude this chapter, I will now turn to how the aesthetic of barrage-style video has circulated around East Asia and developed into its own mode of viewing in a specific regional media network.

The rise of barrage video in East Asian fits into a larger pattern of how televisual culture has worked its way into online media. Indeed, one of the subthemes of this book so far has been the affinity between television and internet media. The relationship between variety television and internet video is worth attending to in detail once more before we move toward topics related to gaming media. Many early studies of internet culture analyzing sites such as YouTube have argued for a break with the televisual in favor of some new rhetoric of media culture. In the case of media such as Niconico and 2channel we can instead observe continuities in the modes of audience spectatorship that circulate between television and online media. Or, perhaps more obviously, we can even use online video sharing to archive televisual media. As such, rather than arguing for "newness" in these so-called new media we might instead consider the similarities they share with television in terms of their place in a more general media environment that allows for such continuities to incubate and transform.[21]

The remediation of internet media into television and movement of staff and talent between television and internet industries is also significant in many cases, such as the reliance on internet video in television news, something that was especially relevant in the immediate aftermath of the March 11, 2011, triple disaster in northeastern Japan. But keeping with this book's focus on the cultural practices associated with online anonymity and spectatorship, this section will also deal with notions of media practice, performance, and vision and how these contribute to a more general sense of a cultural logic or visual syntax of contemporary media.

To rephrase a question posed in the introduction, can television be characterized as a kind of center for the media environment of contemporary Japan? This does not require us to think that all media cultures and practices come out of the television industry or are somehow aesthetically, culturally, or economically, subordinate to television. This notion might instead help us to think of various kinds of media as part of a constellation of forms and practices that move through and intersect in the cultural and technological space of television. In that sense, this centrality is perhaps more literal in terms of how popular music relies on television economically, for its promotion, whether through the coupling of a new single with the latest drama or the incorporation of musical performance in a talk show or variety show. There is also the case of the film industry, which increasingly relies on television for funding and draws on successful television dramas for material. There are also more-abstract, less-economic-focused connections, such as ways audiences develop forms of laughing at embedded visual cues in things like variety TV graphic projection systems. As chapter 5 will discuss in detail, these have been reimagined in "let's play" videos and similar online video media through related modes of presentation and stances of watching as if together as part of a group. In other words, television can appear as the center of contemporary media not just in terms of its economic and institutional power but also in the way it provides a cultural logic of structuring content and developing audience behavior and styles of watching.[22]

There are also cases where television has appropriated visual and formal elements from internet media. This could be viewed as reversing this notion of centering, but it can also be taken as a sign of how that relationship might be requalified. The short-lived variety show *Yonpara: Future Battle* (TBS 2011–12) offers an unusual case for developing a conceptual approach to the relationship between post-nineties *telop* (television opaque projector) systems and the aesthetics of the comment feed on Niconico. It demonstrates multiple registers of appropriation of new media by television and shows how the continued circulation of familiar forms such as graphic projection systems constantly refer to and expand on previous iterations. As with previous topics such as summary sites for 2channel and repeated comments on Niconico, this is part of an aesthetic logic of accumulation.

*Yonpara* is a game-oriented chat program featuring five performers. These performers include the comedian Gekidan Hitori, who appears in a studio location while acting as the master of ceremonies for the show, and four idol-contestants (all members of the now-defunct, all-female, pop music group Not Yet), who appear in separate locations. The host asks questions and introduces quick games for the other performers to engage with, orienting the content around chatter between them and their reactions to the results of each game. Each participant on the show appears in a separate window on the screen and participates on the show via the video-conferencing program Skype. When one participant speaks, that person may take up the full frame for a moment, but for the most part the show uses a picture-in-picture format to show all five faces at once. Conducting the show via Skype is itself an unusual format choice, but what is also striking about the show's presentation is its use of a graphic projection system that appears identical to the scrolling comments of Niconico. Rather than having captions, subtitles, or other kinds of text that appear as in most variety shows, the text in this show scrolls over the screen from left to right, moving at a speed similar to the barrage-style comments of Niconico and even in a font that recalls that used on the website. These will frequently comment on the action depicted in the video, such as the image in figure 4.1, in which a bowling alley is seen and text "comments" describe a strike thrown by own of the performers as a "miracle" and with an exaggerated *kaomoji* (emoticon). The show is, however, not a live broadcast, so these titles are not coming from audiences watching and commenting at home. They are, like conventional *telop* or "canned laughter" of offstage staff, added by the show's production staff to add an additional pseudo-social element of to the experience of watching.[23]

**FIGURE 4.1.** In this bowling-related scene from *Yonpara: Future Battle* (TBS, 2011–12), a strike on the first attempt is followed by enthusiastic "comments" via graphic display projection and the show's contestants. From top to bottom: "Miracle!" "An unbelievable strike." "Awesome!" "Bravo!"

Using a simulation of Niconico's comment feed in lieu of a regular graphic projection system suggests a few points about media convergence. The first is that Niconico's design had become familiar enough a part of visual culture at the time of the show's airing to be viewed as available for appropriation and recognizable by a television audience, which in turn indicates some level of the website's increased presence in the mediascape of Japan. The second is that the circulation of forms between disparate media contribute to a more general sense of visual syntax and media logic shared by discrete forms. This is one way to think about the relationship between televisual and internet media and the ways that different practices or visual styles, familiar tropes, and recognizable affects are cited, simulated, and circulated.

The use of Skype to connect the five participants can be thought of as a continuation of a trend of incorporating social media in television, a trend that has been unfolding in Japan and elsewhere. Twitter and Facebook have found their way into all manner of TV content, including almost everything from TV news featuring Twitter messages posted by politicians to music programs using fan questions to prompt discussions with quests. The music variety show *Coming Soon!* (TBS, 2011–12) was one of the first programs in Japan to use social media messages on air. These were employed alongside the its original purpose of showcasing and promoting the latest releases from commercial musicians. Incorporating Twitter posts by audience members into its graphic projection feed provided a simple way of creating a sense of interactive connectivity between audiences and media. Audiences could react and respond as they watched and then see their messages shown at the end of a performance. In some cases they also had their Tweets read on their air or responded to by the host of the show, Nakai Masahiro.

However, where *Yonpara* differs from a show like *Coming Soon!* is in how the presentation of the show was modeled to make it appear as if the audience's television screen was part of the chat-window for Skype, suggesting that they were also dialed in to the conversation between the show's participants. As part of this presentation, audiences would see the phone icons of the stars ring as they were logging on to the program as the show was starting, and the windows in the screen were organized in a way that was highly reminiscent of a group-chat session. The structure—having the participants speak to the web-cameras affixed to their computers and address one another in friendly, familiar tones—also helped to suggest an atmosphere of intimacy that the viewer could vicariously engage in.[24] There were, of course, many problems with using Skype for the show as well. Image quality in the first few episodes was quite poor, and connection problems resulting in unexpected disconnections, time delays, and video images freezing were common. This could also contribute to the haptic sense of reality of the show and the kind of participatory atmosphere it seemed to be striving for. But there were also criticisms made about the quality of the show by online fans, and the reliability of the connections and quality of the video feed improved considerably during the show's short run.

The use of Niconico-style barrage comments scrolling over the Skype image is another way to consider how a sense of virtual community and watching "together" is suggested through the show's presentation. However, there is also a key difference between the use of Skype and the suggestion of a Niconico-style commenting system. The use of Skype in the show is a case of remediation, in that it is literally incorporated into the show, while the barrage-style comments are actually a simulation of a familiar media form and not an actual incorporation of that media into the new object. Lev Manovich stresses this distinction in his essay on hybridity in computer media, where he notes that "the computer does not 'remediate' particular media . . . rather, *it simulates all media*."[25] This is an important differentiation to make because each process points to a different way that new media are converging toward television and how those processes contribute to the accumulation of a general aesthetic. The remediation of Skype maintains a technological separation in which the software does not become subordinate to television. The simulation of Niconico's comment feed on the show suggests a taming of that media, in which it becomes appropriated and subordinated to the graphic projection system of television and the demands of a noninteractive media. The show borrows from the visual rhetoric and recognizable cultural properties of the comment feed, but it is using that media form on its own terms and not actually engaging with Niconico's website.

Inverse forms of the logic can be seen in the ways that the online video-sharing sites FC2, AcFun, Bilibili, and Mio Mio have begun integrating Niconico-style comments into their video displays. These are still examples of simulation in that they are not actually using Niconico and are instead trying to reproduce the effect of the comment feed through related technologies. This is complicated further in the sense that the comments are being added to commercial television content that has been appropriated and added to the site by its users. In other words, the comments on these sites are like those on Niconico, in that they are added to the video image by users of the site through its interface, but they borrow that aesthetic form (and in the case of AcFun, Bilibili, and Mio Mio, the entire interface and presentation) and incorporate it toward their own purpose, hosting commercial video content. In this sense, these sites threaten to requalify the centrality of television in Japanese media again by remediating TV content for their own purposes but still follow a visual syntax and interface logic that has already been introduced. They combine the aesthetics of accumulation and transmission with those of simulation and remediation.

This in turn suggests another category of how media can invoke an experience that simulates watching or playing together. In addition to viewers of *Yonpara* feeling as if they might be watching with a wider audience, through the comments, or even listening in on an internet phone call through the Skype presentation, the Nico-style comments overlay multiple forms of media experience that suggests watching television and internet media as if they were part of the same screen. This quality of ambivalent co-presence is central to many of the practices analyzed in this book, and this notion will be taken up in greater detail in the next chapter, concerning game-related video and streaming. Different kinds of experience and sensation are encoded as if belonging to various regimes of time, space, and communication, which suggests new ways of thinking about problems of representation and the social in online media. But these are also encoded in a more general syntax of layering of images on top of one another, which are made to appear visually synchronic and available to the viewer in processes of unfolding and visual scanning and browsing. This includes the use of windows showing multiple images within a single frame, such as the integration of Skype chat into Yonpara, and the planarity of the layers of the image expressed by the movement of text over the video screen.

If we think of the layering of images on top of one another as part of a more general logic of cacophony in Niconico and its derivatives, *Yonpara* points to multiple registers of this aesthetic. We can observe this through the way its visual design mobilizes an interstitial aesthetic and how its simulation of social media communication mirrors the social forms of online communication discussed throughout this book. Simulation, as with many of the other forms of media adaptation discussed, both produces something new and is caught between two previously existing forms. This dynamic between emergence and ambivalent betweenness is one of the key characteristics of barrage aesthetics, and we will investigate it further in the following chapter.

# 5

# SCRIPTED LAUGHTER

Um, where is it?

> That one

Ah, this one? It's not there

> "It's not there" (' • ω • ')
> The weapon menu

Uh . . . which is it?

> WEAPON MENU

What should I do? I don't know

> Pay attention!
> You need to really look, lol

It's still not showing up

> Search harder!
> How about actually looking for it
> Search more carefully, lol

The above exchange is taken from a recorded play-through of the video game Metal Gear Solid 4 (Kojima 2008) that was uploaded to Niconico on June 23, 2010. This dialogue consists of narration spoken by the player (shown in roman font) and written reactions produced by the audience watching her progress in

101

the comment feed (shown in italics). The scene is one in which the player struggles to find the item she needs in order to succeed in a confrontation with a boss character at the end of a level. The audience watching the video makes jokes about the obvious location of the weapon in the game-character's inventory, poking fun at the player's obliviousness as she stumbles through the encounter. As described in chapter 1, the comments on Niconico are projected onto the video display screen alongside the video content in scrolling columns of text, meaning that users of the site see the messages written by other members of the audience as they watch along. However, these messages are not from a simultaneous broadcast in which the audience watches the player progress through the game live. They were, rather, posted while the users watched the completed, already uploaded video days, weeks, or even years after the recording had been finished and added to the site. These messages were then added to the video's comment memory to be viewed by other users later.

Given all of this, it is obvious that the comments directed toward the player and her experience in the game cannot influence what is happening in the video. Yet, despite this disparity in time between the initial recording and the post-upload viewing(s), there remains a significant community of users who post comments that seem to be enthusiastically offering encouragement or criticism of what they see in the video. Perhaps, then, there is another social dimension of viewing that these users engage in. By that I refer to the way that although these messages do not reach the player controlling the actions shown in the video, they are still visible to other users of the site. These other users form a parallel audience for the commenting users to perform for and with. This produces an experience of watching together as different users try to make each other laugh by posting messages making fun of the player's difficulties with the game, which then appear as pseudo-synchronous commentary to other viewers. Heavily mediated forms of watching, laughing, and playing emerge out of this dynamic, which we might characterize as an intersection of accumulated user experiences, the asynchronous representations of time provided by the site's design, and the composite media form produced by the addition of comments over the video recording.

This layering of meta-interactive content between different types of users will be the focus of this chapter. The constant adding of new messages to the video's comment feed continually requalifies what the video's identity is as a textual object. With each new set of comments, the experience of viewing changes, sometimes dramatically so. This suggests a shift away from understanding media as a single, discernible object and toward an ongoing process or series of practices that can never be settled. New comments produce new meanings that in turn reorient the status and form of the video away from its original content. That sense of meaning is instead located in the meta-interactive sites of contact between the video and user-produced messages.[1] There is, in other words, something strikingly ambivalent about these videos, even as they seek to capture the attention of their audience. As such, "ambivalence" here refers not only to the sense of being between things in how new meanings are produced by the way the messages augment the video image, but also in how the signification of the video itself is constantly being remade through the messages that appear over it.

Following along with this conceptual arrangement of ambivalence in media and meta-interactive performance, this chapter will analyze online video content that incorporates footage from video game play. The focus will be split between "let's play"–style recordings of video game walkthroughs and playthroughs (often called *jikyō geemu* or *jikyō purei* in Japanese) and livestreaming video (*haishin*) images of gameplay. These genres of online video media have gained cult-like popularity on sites such as YouTube, Twitch.tv, AcFun, and Niconico, adding to the development of new forms of micro-celebrity that have emerged from online media.[2] These types of videos can bring into relief some more general issues related to media form and culture, especially in terms of how they are consumed within the climate of social atomization and how ideas of play have been reimagined in that context.

There are many styles of gameplay videos within the general category of "let's play." Some of these are walkthroughs that show how to progress through difficult parts of games, reveal hidden content, or explain different paths through a game or conclusions to one. Others are live tournament matches between players competing for a prize or title. However, beyond this instructional or competitive motivation, many video makers also engage the audience and invite different modes of feedback or participation through voice-over narration, picture-in-picture representation of the player in the video display (sometimes called "face-cam"), or the use of subtitles and other forms of annotation presented in overlay on the video. As such, in addition to displaying or transmitting skill or knowledge about a specific game, these videos also lend themselves to a mode of performance (often vocal) and structure of engagement with the audience.

With those qualities in mind, although the media genre that this chapter will focus on will entail different types of video images of gameplay, the analytic focus of the argument will largely be on the circuit of meta-interaction between players and audiences. The different ways these interactions are embedded in the video texts and their discursive environments will also be used to analyze this sense of pseudo-reciprocal action between different types of users. One point of emphasis will be the routines of comedic performance that audiences assume when making joking remarks or critical judgments about a player(s). In the case of Niconico and Japanese-language videos on YouTube, many of the roles that players and audiences of these videos assume are borrowed from Japanese variety television, which has a long history of developing general types of roles within a gag structure or routine of banter between comedians. Beyond this connection, the comment feed on Niconico also allows for the kind of paratextual commentary that resonates with the graphic projection systems (*telop*) that have become a staple of variety TV programming in Japan and other parts of East Asia. As such, rather than posing this type of meta-interaction as producing a distinctly new kind of laughter or a new way of viewing, this chapter will instead situate the appearance of iconic laughter in online sociality within more general trends in contemporary media culture in and around Japan.

## Ugly Irony

As the opening example from Metal Gear Solid 4 suggests, the types of performance this chapter is interested in are those that engage with comedic teasing as an audience watches along with a player or performer. To return to the similarities between online media and television in Japan, watching as if together will be taken up as an important quality of spectatorship in this type of media and the various modes of viewing and laughing that they invite. In the case of Niconico, the ironic exchanges written in the comment feed will be related to television variety-comedy and familiar tropes borrowed from established comedic genres. Media critics in Japan have frequently commented on the resemblance between 1980s variety television and contemporary internet culture in Japan, and this chapter will develop some of those observations in regard to certain modes of laughing and watching as if together in semi-reciprocal routines of performance.[3]

There remains, however, one final dynamic of ambivalence in these types of videos. As a complement to this linking between television and internet media through the circulation of performance types (that of *manzai*-influenced television variety-comedy), we should also acknowledge the general rigidity of these kinds of exchanges, which repeat familiar routines seemingly without end. That sense of repetition is presented in a way that appears spontaneous despite often being familiar, with regularly circulated ways of joking and laughing, almost to the point of having a template that is being followed. Therefore, while the media itself might be constantly changing and evolving as new viewers interact with it (such as by adding new comments), the types of interactions being made are in a way resisting that dynamism. The constant rewriting of comments that will repeatedly change a video's presentation is therefore also constant in insisting on a particular way of laughing and distributing those ways of laughing among its participants, with the player as *boke* (fool or clown figure) and audience as *tsukkomi* (admonisher or foil).

Sianne Ngai's conceptualization of "ugly feelings" as a kind of ambivalence in how agency is experienced in the relationship between art and society under late capitalism can serve as a guide for analyzing this dynamic. Borrowing from Ngai's work, this chapter will approach "let's play" videos as "ugly" in their production of laughter through constant repetition that would seem to offer liberating potential for media, by disrupting the settled form of the media object itself, but simultaneously reproduce the same constellations of interactions over and over as users rewrite messages on top of one another (Ngai 2007). The ugly ambivalence of "let's play" videos is therefore split between multiple fronts. There is dividing of agency between the player onscreen and the commenters watching, which in turn informs ambivalence in how these videos resist any one final or definitive form through constant revision and transformation. That ambivalence can also be observed in the style of laughter that is always the same but tries to appear spontaneous and original. The intersection between these qualities of ambivalence produces a sense of rigidity and a culture of viewing that can feel scripted. This is meant not as dismissive but to qualify the ways of viewing and laughing that might be seen as defining the culture around these videos. This also can help identify what is so attractive about these videos and how they signify something of the sensation of watching together that has spread through so many media forms in contemporary visual culture.

Following some of Ngai's insights about "ugly feelings," I am interested in how the routines of repetition and pseudo-rapport found on Niconico that are derivative of television comedy form a sort of script. In an anonymous, asynchronous media culture, this script offers resolution (or faux resolution) of the desire for association in a socially atomized, digital age. I am also interested in how the divergent regimes of representation between the (voiced) performer and (silent) audience are made to feel more proximate. As with many of the other elements of textually cacophonous media described in this book (such as mistyping and characterful expressions of language), I see this dynamic as representing the way cultural forms and media practices under capitalism frequently offer diminished alternatives to existing experiences of social connection (face to face and other), repackaged with novel forms of spectacle to make them more attractive.

## Economies of Play

A "let's play" video is a recording of gameplay using footage captured from a home console system, a mobile device, or a personal computer. The means by which these videos or streams are produced has changed considerably since their initial appearance. In the past, many users would simply point a camera at the television screen they were using to play the game.⁴ This method remains in some cases, but increasingly sophisticated ways of recording have been devised with the arrival of new technologies such as capture cards and streaming. Production values have similarly increased as these types of videos have become more and more popular. For most consoles of recent generations, such as the PlayStation 3 and Xbox One and onward, direct recording onto an external memory drive via a capture card is quite simple to perform, while computer-based emulation is often used to simulate older-generation consoles.⁵ This is also true for many handheld systems, which do not always have the output jack needed to link to a recording unit. When recording a video for a console-based game, a capture card is usually needed to convert the gameplay footage into a separate video file, although the PlayStation 4 and Xbox One consoles (both available since 2013) have included built-in options that can reproduce this ability to record or stream on sites such as Twitch.tv. For computer-based games, videos can be made through software that is run simultaneously with the game. This greatly simplifies the process of recording, although in some cases this can create problems during recording due to the additional memory required by the recording software.

But what is it that is so appealing about these videos to their audience? Most "let's play" videos include some sort of commentary or narration by the player(s) that accompany the footage of gameplay. This is an important dimension that distinguishes these videos from other types of gameplay content such as walk-throughs, playthroughs, and speedruns. Indeed, the "let's" in "let's play" points to this difference in that there is an implication of playing together with the audience, who is not only watching the player(s) but also being addressed by them. We might also understand this as a form of encoding an experience of playing and watching together through the mode of address taken up by the player through his or her vocal performance and how the audience responds through written comments. These commentaries can be made live during the recording of gameplay or edited into the video file after the fact as post-commentary, and some users combine both to create smooth narration and balance the content of their voice-over. There are also variations in the general frame of "let's play," such as "blind" videos in which the player makes a recording of his or her first experience playing a game, or livestreams of gameplay that allow the audience to comment along as the player takes on the game in real time.

"Let's play" videos on YouTube are likely known to many readers due to their explosion in popularity in the 2010s. Similar videos exist on barrage-style videos sites such as AcFun and Niconico, and the integration of comments into the video display intensifies the experience of watching together through its meta-interactive properties. This sensation is difficult to reproduce on YouTube, with its organization of comments, external to the video and hard to view in the same screen.⁶ That said, the introduction of live broadcasting to YouTube, Facebook and Twitch.tv (as well as related sites such as UStream and Hitbox.tv) has brought proximity in experience between these sites due to the way reactions of other viewers have become visible and integrated into the display of the video player. Users can now sense other members of the audience watching along at the same time, and because YouTube relies on account-specific handles for users (which are visible to others), the sense of chatter is much different from the unattributed comments that appear on Niconico or AcFun.

Comments for YouTube videos also appear quite differently depending on whether they are for a livestreamed video or for one that has been recorded and uploaded to the site. Recorded videos have a bulletin-board-like column of user comments that appear beneath their video display. These comments are static. Live broadcasts, however, are accompanied by a comment window that appears adjacent to the video display. In these the comments do move, and newer comments push older messages out of the highlighted feed in a moving scroll of text. The chat window on Twitch.tv is similar in that it is a constantly scrolling series of individual messages, and as with YouTube these comments are presented in a distinct window separate from the display screen of the gameplay content. Even in the case of livestreams on YouTube and Twitch, the video images and the comments are presented diachronically rather than synchronically, so integration is not as strong between the user messages and video comment. Watching the video and reading the comments might be distinct actions in different ways for each site.

We might then conclude that the comments on YouTube are less immediate in their reactions and more totalizing in their address to the uploader or other readers. The sense of ambivalence that they instill might therefore also be less pronounced than that of Niconico or other barrage-style sites. But if we look at the time signature for some comments posted to videos, we can also see that users will post reactions as they are watching. And in some cases they post messages before they could have finished watching the video, such as in the case when a comment is posted immediately after a video has been uploaded and made available for viewing. Both YouTube and Niconico have users who try to race for the "first" comment in a freshly uploaded video, often posting a variation on "first!" or *ichi come* (first comment). It might then be inferred that there is—at least for some users—a kind of enactment of immediacy in commenting on the videos. This recalls Hamano's description of the way posting on 2channel is sometimes organized in anticipation of the thread being locked or deleted. The rush to "get in" while one can has its own type of relation to time (Hamano 2008a, 223–24).

The sensation of liveness or "as if" togetherness is important to each site but perhaps in different ways and to different degrees. As previously mentioned, the very genre of "let's play" videos is distinguished from other types of gameplay recordings in part by this. YouTube's manner of organizing the video display and user comments might not appear to allow that mode of watching or appreciating videos (at least in comparison to Niconico or live broadcasts on Twitch), but users of the site do appear to find ways of enjoying this kind of experience of watching. And even in the case of videos watched on Niconico, the experience of simultaneity is not literally true, even while a sense of pseudo-synchronicity is strong. But as in the example of the recording of gameplay of Metal Gear Solid 4 at the beginning of the chapter, this organization of virtual time also allows for a meta-interaction with the video content and, in the case of videos with user-performers, the performer who appears in the video.

The following section will approach this quality of meta-interactivity in online video within a dialogue, in view of more general trends in contemporary media culture. In the case of game-related content on Niconico, this will involve turning to the relationship between variety television and online media. Focusing on the circulation of comedic performance routines and the experience of watching together that might be suggested through the incorporation of text into the visual design of televisual media, we can observe some of the ways that watching "as if" together and the "ugly" forms of laughter in these videos have grown out of variety television spectatorship.

## Watching Together

As mentioned above, one of the key features of the videos discussed in this chapter is the feeling of watching alongside an audience. Listening to the voice of the player as they progress through the game and narrates his or her actions might suggest the experience of watching over the shoulder of the player, while reading the comments of other viewers on Niconico and other barrage-media sites invites a feeling of liveness via the experience of virtual simultaneity. The relationship between these modes of watching and the various performances of laughter on display in user-made comments is another point to consider in understanding how these parasocial forms of media consumption are encoded and enjoyed. This section will take up the possibility of an ironic stance in watching that is part of a circuit of meta-interactive, semi-reciprocal modes of watching and performance. We will begin by focusing on Niconico and its connection with variety television of the 1980s and 1990s before moving on the YouTube, Twitch.tv, and their place in global internet culture. The goal will be to draw out how each media environment has its own distinct practices of laughter and irony that intersect with one another through shared genres such as "let's play" videos.

A common sight on contemporary television in Japan is a panel of commentators and comedians watching a VTR (video tape recording) on a monitor, often appearing as floating heads as a picture-in-picture to offer reactions as they watch virtually along with the audience at home. This suggestion of performers in the program and spectators viewing the program from elsewhere sharing the experience of watching is used in all types of genres, ranging from "wide show" programs that mix news and entertainment to "infotainment" programs about local or foreign cultural peculiarities. Most relevant for our discussion is how prank- and humor-oriented programs use these devices to allow for the audience to laugh along with the comedians who are in on the joke at the expense of the presumably unknowing rube. The double vision of watching content of a video while simultaneously following along extradiegetic commentary in a TV show can be compared to the way Niconico users watch both the video content and the commend feed. Both models incorporate different registers of visual information within the same frame, and these layers of content often comment on one another or add meaning. In the case of television, this mode of commentary is, of course, often auditory in addition to being textual, whereas the comment feed on Niconico is only visual. We can still consider some of the ways these practices of commentary and layering of information intersect with one another in order to develop some connections between acts of watching and popular forms of comedic performance and discourse in Japan.

Kitada Akihiro has identified the Nihon Television variety show *TV That Will Make You Laugh* (*Genki ga deru terebi*, Nihon TV, 1984–96) as the progenitor of this format of "shared watching" by comedians and TV audiences in variety programs (Kitada 2005, 157–61). The show used a pseudo-documentary setup to have non-comedians (put in unusual situations or locations) become subject to ridicule and jest by the TV talent and performers observing them via monitor from the studio. This led to the feeling of an enormous in-joke in which the audience assumes a stance similar to that of the performers on the show due to their sharing of a privileged position of knowledge and their special vision. Borrowing the language of *manzai* comedy, Kitada claims that the amateur being subjected to the jokes fulfills a role like the *boke* (clown or fool) while the comedians on-screen and the audience at home assume the role of the *tsukkomi* (chastising figure).[7] However, rather than laughing at jokes produced in conventional fashion such as wordplay or observational humor, this kind of laughter is instead what Kitada calls of "sneering" laughter, part of an "irony game" that is based on assumption of a "pseudo-superior" position to that of the would-be *boke*.[8] Two qualities that this in-joke-oriented mode of watching might share with the presentation of the comment feed on Niconico is the sense of watching from a removed, privileged position (as a kind of ironic or comedic stance) and the significance of the monitor screen as a mediating force.

"Let's play" videos on Niconico rarely feature the same kind of visual representation of the player. This is due in large part to local conventions around *kaodashi* (showing one's face), which has not been the normal mode of representation on Niconico the way it is for video-sharing sites such as YouTube and Twitch.tv or even social media services like Facebook and Instagram. There are, however, frequently voice-over narrations that imply a similar kind of panel that is playing or watching together, which can then be thought of as providing another kind of in-group that the user visiting the site can watch along with in the same way that Kitada argues that television audiences experience with variety TV.[9] This is also not uncommon in English-language videos and streams on YouTube and Twitch. But the main element through which this sense of watching along with others is conveyed is the unique properties of the site's comment feed. The way that virtual experiences of time are initiated and performed was addressed in greater detail in chapter 1, but in gameplay videos the feeling of pseudo-synchronicity is buttressed by the performance of character types similar to the constellation of *boke* and *tsukkomi* that Kitada finds in variety TV programming.

As described in the example from Metal Gear Solid 4 at the beginning of the chapter, this most often appears through joking commentary addressed to the player of the game as if the commentary was live, at the same time as the play. The users who write these comments are perfectly aware of the virtual form of time on the site and that the player cannot read or respond to their comments, so the mode of address is not one of literal, direct communication but rather one that produces a sense of meta-interaction with the content of the video to create a comedic circuit of laughter for other viewers to appreciate and laugh at. The sense of watching together in these videos is thus not just about experiencing a sensation of watching as part of an audience but also about finding new ways of laughing that are produced through the sense of meta-interaction between the video performer and the commenting audience members.

In these videos the distribution of *boke* and *tsukkomi* roles between the player and audience are thus not only something that users come to understand through the circulation of similar forms in televisual media like variety-comedy. They are also an emerging circuit of exchange that has developed around the structure of the site and its possibilities of meta-interactivity. This can also extend to the different ways the performer and audience solicit laughter from one another. The player or uploader can provide content that can be taken up by other users later, so the assumption of a *boke*-like stance is somewhat naturalized by the limitations of their mode of participation. The content of the video cannot change after it has been added to the site, and a player's performance cannot be revised once the video has been added. As such, the solicitation of laughter through routines of failure or silliness that invite the audience to make fun of players is an easy way to initiate a circuit of pseudo-reciprocal play and performance. The "ugliness" of these videos might appear to be in how so many of these jokes are made at the expense of the player as *boke*, but we might also consider that it is actually in the rigidity of the routines of laughter that we can find the kind of ambivalent ugliness that Ngai has described.

The post-upload commentary is, of course, more flexible since there are no such limitations on time of input. Users can post outrageous, *boke*-style comments that invite other users to make fun of them as easily as they can ironic, *tsukkomi*-style messages. That said, the culture of anonymity on the site and the familiar routines of reciprocal performance encourage the *tsukkomi* mode of making joking commentary on these videos.[10] Site users' familiarity with variety television performance routines also encourages this type of construction of meta-routines between audiences and performers. On top of that, while the meta-interaction between the onscreen performer and the comment feed might be seen as re-creating the *boke* and *tsukkomi* routine of laughter, the design of the comment feed also produces a similar sense of a spectatorship, of watching from a privileged position of an extradiegetic space, one that bridges the experience of the viewer watching at home to the content of the performance through a sense of meta-proximity.

The resemblance between variety television graphic display systems and the comment feed on Niconico is another way of considering this circulation of performance routines and the kind of vision these media suggest. Ota Shoichi's writing on the graphic projections systems from Japanese variety TV of the 1990s provides a useful approach for thinking about Niconico's comment feed and its relationship to this kind of meta-interactive performance of *tsukkomi*-like routines of laughter and ironic, sneering humor.[11] As with the kinds of comments described at the beginning of the chapter from the video of Metal Gear Solid 4, television projection systems will sometimes take up the role of the mocking, admonishing half of the *manzai* comedy performance duo. These images and text will make fun of the onscreen performers or content from a removed "space" (*kuukan*) that is visually available to the audience at home but not for the performers on camera. There is an overlap between this presentation and the in-joke structure of the shared viewing Kitada describes, which Ota calls a "space of friendship" (*nakama no kuukan*). Beyond the parallels in producing laughter through captioning and visual cues, the overflowing, layered presentation of text over the image and the transformation of written discourse into a figural image are other ways the aesthetics of variety *telop* have been echoed in Niconico comments.

The difference between these types of captioning systems and that of the Niconico comment feed is that these subtitles and other graphic projection images are not being produced by another member of the audience. They are instead being added by the makers of the show to complement or add structure to the banter between performers and their routines. The comments on Niconico are perhaps still removed from the experience of the viewer in the sense that they have been added outside of his or her immediate experience with the media. But there is also an acknowledgement of another productive viewer that is participating in the same social register of other video-watching users on the site. In this sense the experience of meta-interaction is quite different, in that while a Niconico user can post messages as if communicating with the onscreen performance, the mode of participation suggested in Ota's reading of variety *telop* is one in which audience members who laugh together via the suggestion of a space for laughter in the graphic projection feed are not leaving a trace of their own engagement with that media. Similarly, the text in variety *telop* is fixed, while the comments on Niconico can change as new messages are input by users and replace older comments.

There is perhaps a related kind of virtual space of participation made available through the way both media expand the visual content of a video or television show using extradiegetic graphics that augment or transform the onscreen image. The use of text layered over the primary image in both cases suggests different ways of thinking about how processes of re-inscription, repetition, and augmentation produce new ways of laughing, of feeling as if watching or laughing together. Recalling the concept of ambivalence, this space of participation also intersects with the media object in a way that produces something new but perhaps still subordinate to the original videotext. Chapter 2 identified some of the practices of "double vision" that visitors of Niconico might encounter through the site's comment feed, but the way variety *telop* and video comments both suggest virtual experiences of time through text that anticipates onscreen content is another node through which a sensation of active engagement through laughter might be produced.

As mentioned previously, many websites do not feature the same type of interface that foregrounds the presence of other users. "Let's play" videos on YouTube and Twitch sometimes produce a mode of watching together by having more than one voice present in the narration or having a picture-in-picture of the player with a friend or helper beside him. For example, some YouTube videos feature two or three performers, with one assuming the role of player (which typically includes providing commentary for the game) and the others joining in to make fun of the player with ironic jabs about mistakes or moments of failure. Streamers on Twitch will also frequently hold multi-stream broadcasts in which different channels connect through internet telephone and voice-chat software (such as Discord), allowing for a feeling of casual sociality to go along with the images of gameplay. And although part of a media environment different from Niconico or Japanese variety TV, the distribution of roles in these videos are often very similar. One member will appear as a clown figure to be made fun of, while the others tend to be more aloof and ironic, cuing the audience as how to laugh along with the developing routine. As with the presence of a player's voice, this sense of rapport between an onscreen panel (or joint voice-over, in the case of channels that do not show the faces of their players) implies a mode of laughing and invitation for the audience to laugh, encoding a meta-intimate sense of proximity with the performer.

Many of the most popular YouTube content producers who make "let's play" videos also employ face-cam, allowing for a picture-in-picture representation that shows their own face in a windowed section within the section on the screen. Indeed, the addition of one's face to the video is deeply ingrained with routines of fame and celebrity on YouTube (as well as Twitch). This also provides a sharp contrast to the invisibility of players on Niconico and its far more intense environment of anonymity and micro-celebrity. Videos that feature face-cam will frequently show exaggerated reactions to events in the game, providing visual cues for the audience as to how to perceive the video content, further cementing the celebrity of the player-performer. However, in addition to the dynamic of anonymous, invisible audience members watching a visualized player, the use of face-cam is often part of an embellishment of the commentary voice-over.

## Televisual Prototype

We should return to variety television in Japan as a key intertext for these kinds of videos. The relationship this chapter is trying to draw between variety TV and internet videos of gameplay is perhaps best embodied by Fuji Television's *GameCenter CX* (2003 to present). In this show the comedian Arino Shinya (from the comedy duo Yoiko) assumes the role of a staff member from a game company who rises in rank depending on his success at completing older-generation video games, typically within a set time limit of twenty-four hours. Many of the games he is forced to play are notoriously difficult classics such as Ghosts 'n Goblins (which are often called "brutish" or *kichiku* games by fans), so the humor of the show comes from Arino's repeated failures (which audience can presumably identify with based on their own experience), his reactions to getting stuck in the games, and the support or mocking from the show's staff and graphic projection feed. The latter will often ask if he is ready to give up or make notes of the number of times he has failed at a particular challenge.

There are many elements of this show that are similar to other forms of variety TV discussed by Ota and Kitada. For example, the use of ADs (assistant directors) and other staff as characters who interact with the performers has been seen since programs like *We Are the Laugh Tribe* (Fuji, 1981–89), which featured the laughter of the off-camera crew and incorporated the show's director as a character at times. Similarly, the use of graphical text such as *telop* subtitles to supply comedic commentary is reminiscent of other forms of TV variety. One difference to highlight here is the emphasis on failure as a kind of spectacle. Failure in comedy, of course, is not unique to this show. Punishment games (*batsu geemu*) have been a staple of television comedy for years on Japan, with shows like *Gaki no tsukai* (*Gaki no tsukai yarahen de*, NTV 1989 and on) featuring games and challenges in which contestants try not to laugh or try to guess the correct answer to a puzzle based on limited information, with eventual punishment being the main attraction. In the case of *Game Center CX*, the failure at a game is not a prompt for punishment but is rather the content that organizes the show and the way its audience views it. Similarly, because the audience can presumably identify with Arino's experiences at failing at these games, the kind of laughter is perhaps more empathetic than the sadistic kind we might sense in punishment game shows. There is still ugliness in this type of laughter, though, as with Kitada's model of ironic distance, it lies somewhere between cynical meanness and something more empathetic. There is ambivalence, an invitation to the audience to laugh but with laughter distancing the viewer from the performance of the player onscreen.

## Ambivalent Layers of Play

This also leads us to another set of questions: Are these videos a replacement for the experience of playing a game oneself? If so, can watching one of these videos be a different, emerging form of play? We should also consider what specific kinds of pleasures are found in watching these kinds of videos and what kind of activity of viewing their audiences take up. Following those concerns, this section will try to articulate a model for thinking of these videos as instilling a sense of meta-interactivity and emerging forms of play. We might also consider that there is a mode of performance in this type of media that has its own properties of mediation and a register of activity that is distinct from—although perhaps still subordinate to—the games being shown in the videos. In other words, the experience of watching these videos can rather be approached as a case for rethinking what something like play might mean in an environment of meta-interactive, mediated sociality in which the stability of discrete texts is constantly coming undone due to continuous layering of composite forms.

We can begin by looking at some rather unusual examples of "let's play" videos from Niconico, focusing on a single user and that user's audience. Although perhaps not representing what many videos of this style would look like, the type of comment art that is produced by the audience for these videos makes clear the possibility of watching and following as a form of play. Thus, rather than use these cases to represent what "let's play" videos might look like, this section will use them to help introduce their status as ambivalent media forms. It is important to keep in mind that while "let's play" videos are generated from video games, they also become distinct media forms in themselves by turning a single instance of play (a unique temporal act) into a recorded object that is available outside of the normal constraints of time. Furthermore "if let's play" videos are part of the creation of a tangible site of performance and play from the games they employ, the act of watching might also be thought of as initiating a paratextual site of play and performance that is bound to the video but also augments it.

"P-P" is a retired uploader of "let's play" videos on Niconico who has recorded and uploaded dozens of gameplay videos to his channel on the site. Many of these are of older-generation video games, from the 1980s and 1990s, and among the most widely viewed of these are his series of videos in which he plays games from the Super Mario Brothers franchise. The twist in this series is that P-P plays the games with a controller-pad designed to be used with the Dance Dance Revolution (DDR) dancing game. This replaces the normal controller for the console, so instead of playing the games with a hand-held unit, he stands on a flat, plastic sheet that has the various button functionalities mapped onto its surface. P-P therefore plays the game by pressing buttons with his feet rather than his hands, adding a layer of difficulty for him.

This is also incorporated into the presentation of the videos. While the main image shown in the videos is that of the gameplay, as with other "let's play" videos, a window-in-window box in the upper-left corner of the screen shows P-P's body from the waist down, standing on the controller. This allows the audience to follow along with his progress through the game and also see his movements. His clumsiness with the gamepad is readily apparent in the earliest videos in the series, but his movements become much more skillful and coordinated as he gets used to it. As with many other videos of this type, P-P speaks over the images of gameplay, but his commentary feels breathless, more so than most other video producers, as he narrates his every action, reacting to things that go well or end poorly for him, expressing his excitement about overcoming difficult obstacles in the game.

As seen in the chapter-opening example from Metal Gear Solid 4, the Niconico comment feed is commonly used by audience members to make fun of the performer onscreen in the video. Many of these comments address mistakes and struggles with the more difficult parts of the game, which in P-P's case are made even harder by use of a DDR pad instead of a hand-held controller. However, his commentary and narration also become subject to many jokes, with users repeated things he says in the comment feed or performing *tsukkomi*-like jokes that make light of things he says as he tries to succeed at the games. For example, in a video he made of Super Mario 64 (Nintendo 1996), a user begins to count the number of times he repeats "what should I do?" (*dō shi*) when faced with a part of the game that stumps him (fig. 5.1). Similarly, during a video of Super Mario Brothers 3 (Nintendo, 1988), his repetition of the phrase "believe in yourself and press on!" (*jibun wo shinjite ayunde ikō*) prompts one user to write "this is a big deal so he said it twice" (*daiji na koto nanode ni kai imashita*) (fig. 5.2). Another user tops things off by declaring P-P's repeated phrase as "famous words, lol" (*meigen w*). These latter two comments are both standard *tsukkomi*-style phrases and often used in the comment feeds of videos across the site.[12]

These comments making fun of P-P, like those commenting on the Metal Gear Solid 4 video at the beginning of this chapter, were produced after the video was recorded and uploaded. As such, they do not engage in literal interaction between the video maker and audience. There is, however, a tendency or impulse to rehearse these kinds of meta-interactive exchanges and routines of mediated performance. These comments are also meant to be seen by other users and to provoke laughter or other reactions, and this should not be ignored. Not

**FIGURE 5.1.** Users write joking comments over a playthrough of a Mario 64 video game. One counts the number of times the player exclaims "what should I do?"

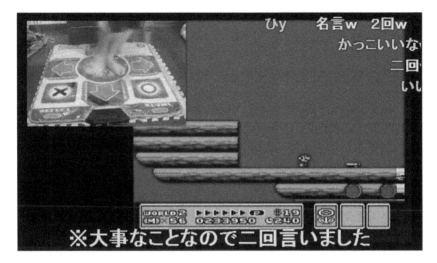

**FIGURE 5.2.** Comment feed for P+P's video of Super Mario Brothers 3 reads "famous phrase" (*meigen*) in response to the player's repetition of "believe in yourself and press on."

all comments, however, are linguistic in their approach to participating in the experience of play. Another example from one of P-P's videos shows some of the other ways audiences of these videos engage with a particular mode of play or participate in ways made possible by the interface of Niconico's comment feed.

As introduced in chapter 2, users of the site called comment artists (*shokunin*) make pixelated sprite-like cartoon images or drawings that they then project and animate across the screen via the scrolling movement of the comment system. With older-generation video games such as Super Mario 3 it is possible to create an image that looks similar to those of the game itself. In figure 5.3 we can see how comment artists have posted things like flying masses of white that resemble clouds as a player moves into a sky-themed level and moving black orbs that look like the bullet-enemies, and they have even added what appears to be new detail in the game-world environment by drawing walls and other obstacles. To other viewers watching these videos on their computers or phones, this type of comment art can make it appear as if the character icon for Mario is about to be hit by an enemy or run into an obstacle in the game. Or, factoring in the awareness of how the comment feed works, they produce the sensation that someone in the comment feed is virtually attacking the player by creating these new sprites to interfere with the player's progress. But as with any other kind of comment, these are added to the video after the recording has already been complete, so there is no possibility of the comment artists' animations actually interrupting P-P's concentration on the game or otherwise making him commit an in-game error.

A related example can be seen in a video of Dead Space (Electronic Arts, 2008) that was made by a user with the handle "Osaka." This particular "let's play" series is part of the *yukkuri* subgenre on Niconico in which the player substitutes his own voice with one created using voice synthesizer software.[13] Part 14 of the series features a moment when the player activates a powerful in-game item, during which he adds a new soundtrack to the video—the theme song from the *tokusatsu* (a type of live action special effects driven television program) television program *Space Sheriff Gavan (Uchuu keiji Gyaban)* (Asahi, 1982–83). The upbeat, silly tone of the song is jarring in the atmosphere of the game, which is a mix of science fiction and horror. There is, however, a slight resemblance between the character that the player controls and the protagonist of the show.[14] The mismatch between the two media is embraced in the comment stream by the audience, who begin to write out the lyrics of the song in bright-colored text that scrolls across the screen as the song plays over images of the game (fig. 5.4). Some comments appear as layers of different-colored text that fly past one another, creating a strange tapestry of moving planes. Other comments appear as static exclamations that pop into view, emphasizing the moment of action or adding weight to a line of dialogue.

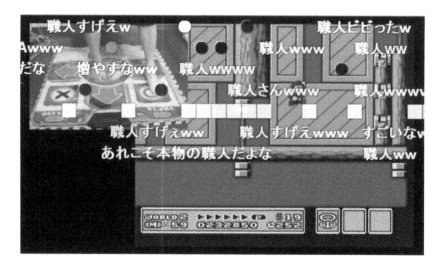

**FIGURE 5.3.** An example of pixel game art in P-P's playthrough of Super Mario Bros 3. The comment art resembles the assets of the game, playing with the notion that the comments are invading its space.

**FIGURE 5.4.** Osaka's playthrough of Dead Space features song lyrics as colorful comments while the song plays.

This is a different kind of meta-interaction than that described in relation to P-P's video of Super Mario 3. The introduction of the song (which Osaka has edited into the soundtrack) provides something of a solicitation or invitation to post comments in response. Adding transcribed lyrics in the comment feed is a popular kind of writing on Niconico, and, as a veteran of the site, Osaka would have been familiar with that style of posting. As such, while the drawing of game-like elements in the comment feed for the Super Mario 3 video is something audience members take up on their own, the comments produced here feel closer to a pseudo-collaboration with the video maker due to the way the comment artists respond to a recognizable cue. In this sense, if the audience writing comments for P-P's videos is creating a paratextual instance of the video by creating pixelated art that resembles the game content, a similar kind of paratextual, interstitial augmentation of the images of gameplay is being jointly produced by both Osaka and Osaka's viewers.

This can actually be thought of as another variation on the cultural aesthetic of "nth order derivative" collaborations on Niconico, a concept sometimes used to describe the way Vocaloid videos are produced by dividing the creative labor (writing music, drawing art, animating the art, etc.) between a number of users.[15] More abstractly, this notion of derivative pseudo-collaboration also relates to how the network sociality of Niconico and its tagging and commenting systems encourage a mode of thinking across individual texts to connections between texts and away from individual moments of authorship to a distributed sense of creation across an aggregate of users. This again suggests the ambivalence of this type of media, in that its mode of production or authorship is located between different users and in that the stability of the video as a discrete media form cannot be located in just the video itself. It requires the overlaying of comments by other users to complete the circuit initiated by the uploader-performer.[16]

## Interface of Layers

It is in this dynamic of meta-reciprocal performance and aesthetic of separation between media forms that these videos can demonstrate interstitiality and ambivalence in textually cacophonous media. If a "let's play" video can animate a game or transform it into an experience of play, this kind of textual meta-interaction can similarly be viewed as transforming the gameplay recording into a new site for activity. It would appear that the precise site of activity is being continuously recentered or mediated further and further from its original form via this continuous process of augmentation.[17] To clarify this, we can think of the initial act of play as animating the game into an isolated experience rendered in time, but the recording of that experience then transforms that act into a media form available to others without the same constraints of time. The act of play becomes archival. Through this series of transformations from game into experience of play and finally into video, the experience of play becomes available for further augmentation through different kinds of participation (labor) on behalf of the audience. This possibility of transformation is where the notion of ambivalence becomes important. These comments become part of a separate, distinct site or space of game-becoming activity, one that can be thought of in terms of producing layers of action and play, layers that are separate (but subordinate) media objects. This is also part of simultaneously producing a new, composite register of meta-interactivity that appears between or within these moments of play.

Alexander Galloway's writing on interface effects points to a similar set of issues. He characterizes the interface as a historically produced phenomenon and notes how economic change throughout the world (specifically change associated with the rise of neoliberalism) has brought about new modes of reading that have become enmeshed in transformations of labor (scanning, sampling, and parsing) that are also part of an evolving, autonomous regime of representation and mode of interaction (Galloway 2012). He asserts that the interface is better described as a process than as a discrete thing or object due to this emphasis on transformation in experiences of proximity and material states they initiate. Galloway's impulse to describe the interface in terms of transformation and its own aesthetic qualities and networked status resonates with this chapter's attempt to characterize these videos as ambivalent. In the continual transfer of the experience of play away from the physical game-object itself and toward the act of watching via its remediation in a video format, one distributed across a networked audience, we can interpret these videos as suggesting ambivalence. This ambivalence is based on their dynamic of being on a threshold between media and the discrete series of practices that emerge from said media. Similarly, the transformation of reading to a kind of labor via new kinds of media consumption also intersects with the way that play might become appropriated as labor in "let's play" videos.

The Niconico comment feed can be readily seen as a kind of interface or interface effect due to its aesthetic design and function, but this notion should also be couched in the tension between individual players and the mass of anonymous (or pseudo-anonymous) spectators they attract. The location of the interface, then, is not just how the technology of the site works in presenting different kinds of information and in facilitating user experience but also in the relationality between different kinds of users and the constellation of roles they take up within that frame. What emerges from this relationship is a series of layers of activity distributed across the user base and positions of watching and playing. This also involves layering of media forms as the original videos become subject to further transformation through the way audiences interact with them. Returning to how an array of media forms encourages different interpretations and arrangements of space and barriers of interaction can prove useful in elaborating on this point.

Video game studies scholars have been arguing over whether the differentiation between diegetic and non-diegetic in approaching things like game music and interfaces is useful. Borrowed from film studies, "diegesis" refers to the environment of the narrative world of the film. The most common use of this term is in describing different sources of sound. Sounds indexical of a source within this space would be referred to as diegetically sourced (such as a band visible in the background of a shot), while sound with a source not-identifiable in the narrative space of the film would be considered non-diegetic (such as a soundtrack or score). The clarity of this distinction has been a subject of debate in film studies, such as Rick Altman's observations about how seemingly non-diegetical music in dance sequences in Hollywood musicals seems to be directing the action of the characters (Altman 1987). Video game critics and scholars have also questioned how clear this distinction can be in games when diegetically sourced sounds or actions are directed at the player, such as a character-sprite in Warcraft 3 asking "more work?" (speaking to no one in the game-space) when prompting a player to do something while the game moves toward "idle" status (Jorgensen 2011). This anxiety about the differentiation of diegetic and non-diegetic spaces and sources in video games is related to their interactive nature and the way that seemingly diegetic content is aimed at directing the player toward certain actions. There is not a clear distinction between these two spaces but still a sense that there are multiple ranges of activity happening across the media's interface. These can also occur simultaneously within the same action, further troubling this distinction. Kristine Jorgensen identifies the "double status" of some sounds in video games through the way they address the player via seemingly diegetically sourced origins, which we can take as a way to begin thinking productively about this.

I don't intend to revive the debate of diegetic/non-diegetic as a productive distinction for thinking about Niconico and its comment feed. However, we might consider that the doubleness Jorgensen notices in video game sound might be a useful starting point in thinking about where and how we might locate the activity of meta-reciprocal play in Niconico recordings. What can be gained from this scholarship then is not so much the vocabulary it introduces (or borrows from film studies) as what that desire for a specialized vocabulary hints at—precision in describing the forms of experience that are opened up through different sorts of media and the cultures of use that appear around them. This is especially true when we approach such media from the perspective of ambivalence, which also suggests betweenness or separation between layers.

For example, if we return to the simulation of games elements such as the blocks of pixels that appear in the comment feed of P-P's playthrough of Super Mario Brothers 3, we might surmise that audiences of these videos can see and interpret comments as a part of the game (in which the video content and comment feed are materials of a more abstract media object) but also perceived them through a double vision that sees and recognizes both the video and the comments as discrete media objects that are layered, one on top of the other. This can perhaps even signal a mode of viewing in which the "video + comments" appear as different iterations of the same proto-object of reified play-activity. The screen surface of the video display is then not only the site for this play-activity but also the site for the activity of reading that animates the game-object(s) for the viewer. What seems important is how watching helps initiate these videos as multiple instances of media and activity: game (the game itself), play (the act of play recorded in the video), and vision (the activity of watching, commenting, and reading comments taken up by the audience).

The example of Niconico comment art is perhaps too unusual a case to make this approach represent other types of user participation. The simulation of sprite-like game elements in the comment feed demonstrates one kind of meta-interactive play (or perhaps multiple forms, in that the interpretation of the comment art as part of the video, not part of the game, is also significant). And recognizing this type of outlier case can help establish the parameters of the kind of media culture we are trying to pin down and what might be at stake in identifying that specific culture of use. But videos on YouTube or Twitch.tv do not intrinsically have such visually spectacular modes of audience participation. There might still be a related potential for networks of play, augmentation, and separation, however, even while the visual arrangements of these sites do not as readily trouble the distinction between diegetic (the original video of gameplay itself) and extradiegetic or paradiegetic (the commentary of the audience projected over the video).

This sense of augmentation can be found most directly in the use of browser extensions and similar types of applications. Twitch Danmaku, a browser extension used while viewing Twitch.tv streams, allows for the messages that have been posted in chat to be projected over the video window in a way reminiscent of Niconico. This is something that individual users have to download and activate on their own, however, since it isn't part of the site's native design interface. It is designed and employed by audiences of the site who wish to simulate the experience of Niconico-style video viewing. That said, some Japanese streamers run this type of application as the default setting for their own streams, meaning that even viewers without the browser extension installed or activated will see comments projected in a way that resembles Niconico's comment system.

The introduction of online gaming services such as Steam (Valve) and the now defunct Games for Windows Live (Microsoft) has added another layer of complexity. These services host games for online play by facilitating player connections or storing game data, but this also means they project new types of paratextual interface elements onto the game. For example, log-on screens appeared across the screen of games hosted by Games for Windows Live, and Steam sends the player messages in the bottom right-hand corner of the screen when a notification has been received. Manipulating these types of paratextual elements has allowed users to interrupt games being streamed live on Twitch.tv by projecting this extradiegetic, menu-originated content onto the screen and sending messages and invitation notifications through the game platform software. This can possibly block game content but generally serves as a nuisance or distraction for the player when sent out en masse.[18]

## Quality of Voice and Quality of Personality

Despite these many differences in apparatus of presentation and the possibilities for meta-interaction they invite, voice-over narration remains one of the key qualities of "let's play" videos across platforms. Some common variations on voice commentary include a running dialogue that explains the content of the game as the player proceeds, frustrated rants about the skill level of other players in online matches, and comedic routines that make fun of the game and invite the audience to laugh along. There are similarly many variations on how the voice of the player or uploader can be heard. Some videos feature only a single voice and player, while others appear as a conversation between players, often with one playing and the other(s) watching. And while many videos feature no visual representation of the player, others anchor the voice to a body through the appearance of the player on a face-cam representation or through a face-tracking application that renders the player as an animated cartoon character, commonly known as a VTuber (Virtual YouTuber). The quality of sound recording of the voice also varies tremendously from video to video. Uploaders aiming for professional quality typically have microphones and sound mixing units dedicated to ensuring clarity, while beginning or hobbyist players rely on consumer-grade headphone-mic sets and record their voice and sounds from the game in a single channel, resulting in less clarity.[19]

Also significant in this emphasis on voice is that only the player is represented this way. Audiences in the Niconico comment feed, Twitch chat stream, and YouTube comments section are represented only through text. Many users attempt to intensify the expressive potential of text by introducing elements such as emoticons and comment art and by copying and pasting different kinds of text and code. That said, in general the players or uploaders have a mode of representation that privileges their status as individual users, whereas audience representation is bound up in their anonymity or pseudo-anonymity and exists in aggregate, less individually recognized form.

We might ask, then, whether this dynamic in representation that each party enjoys reproduces or intersects with the separation of media texts in "let's play" videos. In other words, if we think of "let's play" videos as layered, composite media forms with a pronounced quality of ambivalence, the gap in representation between players and audiences might suggest another kind of interval of media and sensation. It is particularly along the opening of representation between individualized, visible or audible modes of performance or speech and the anonymous, suspended modes of participation in which audiences are active that these questions should be pursued. This opening can be thought of as a difference between privileged and unprivileged modes of representation. The human voice is often characterized as having an indexical quality that points to the body that produces it.[20] But what kind of presence is felt for users who communicate not through their individual voices but instead through columns of text produced by copying and pasting blocks of writing? One way to approach this question would be to look to the quality of intensity in some of these forms of textual discourse. The comment art described earlier in this chapter is one such case, but we can also look to the prevalence of spamming block messages in Twitch chat feeds and the use of emoticons as other ways the aggregate form of membership of the anonymous audience is expressed. This intensely visual technique engages with a mode of representation grounded more in affect than signification.

The spoken voice-over of the players in these videos expresses something of their individual idiosyncrasies and personality. Similarly, because vocal narration is typically performed in a casual, conversational style of speech, it conveys a feeling of spontaneity and even intimacy.[21] Qualities of performance must also be considered, such as in the example from Metal Gear Solid 4 described at the opening of this chapter. The player moves between different tones and character-like stances as she plays, inviting different reactions from the audience as they laugh along with her at the in-game characters or laugh at her as she fails at the task at hand. Indeed, the quasi-invitation to respond to and make fun of the player is partially born out of this meta-intimacy encoded by the voice of the player. In this example, the gender of the player is also relevant and is something she also mobilizes in her performance.[22]

To return to the issue of asymmetry between voice-enabled performer and text-limited audience, the introduction of text-to-speech applications introduces further complexity to this dynamic. It has been mentioned that some video makers use a Vocaloid voice synthesizer instead of their own voice (the *yukkuri* style of "let's play" videos), but some streamers go even further and add a text-to-speech application to the chat window used by the audience, granting them a limited form of vocalization. This is also frequently connected to the use of fully anonymous chat rooms, which are used as a supplement to sites such as Twitch.tv that require permanent accounts. Applications such as UChat can provide a separate, fully anonymous chat window for audience comments. Supplementing that feature with a text-to-voice program such as *Bōyomi-chan* ("monotone-chan") will create the loose feeling of a conversation as the voice synthesizer reads aloud messages entered by spectators off-site. This saves the streamer the trouble of needing to constantly look at the text-chat, but it also introduces that feeling of a casual conversation.

At first glance it would seem that this addition of virtual vocalization can increase the mode of representation that audiences can enjoy while watching a stream. They can leave the realm of text and gain a voice, communicating with the streamer on somewhat equal terms. However, because the text is read aloud by a voice synthesizer, it is not the individual voice of the author that is speaking, and, further, it is being read in the same monotone as every other message entered in that chat window. Users are able to "speak" through the program and address the streamer, but that speech is anonymous and deindividualized. It does not possess the unique qualities or idiosyncrasies we expect of a human voice but rather renders everyone part of the same generalized chatter.

This can return us to the notion of polyphonic noise and chatter that was introduced in chapter 1. However, while that discussion focused on text-based communication on Niconico, the above example represents a more literal quality of polyphonic communication in which voices collide and mash together. Rather than the preservation of distinct voices or subjectivities that Bakhtin and Sakai describe, in these cases authorship is erased and transformed into a redistributed voicing of the aggregate mass. This is not a case of individual voices competing with one another or expressing their own will or subjectivity. The voices becoming an anonymous mass in turn create a communication dynamic essentially between two parties: the streamer and the aggregation of the audience. The audience speaks almost as one collective voice.

Given this pronounced asymmetry in representation between players and audiences, what can help mend this gap? How do different types of users enjoy varying modes of representation while still feeling like they are engaging with and being engaged by a stream or video upload? In writing on studio audience laughter and laugh tracks, Jacob Smith has noted that laughter helps "bridge that gap" between audiences and recorded texts (Smith 2009, 7). Keeping that in mind, laughter can be thought of as producing a sense of presence for an audience and the constellation of performances that appear around them. Thus, posting funny comments on Niconico or Twitch is as much about playing to other viewers as it is about achieving some kind of meta-interaction with the original text. The following section will take this issue up in greater detail, diving into the ways that sensations of watching together are encoded in televisual and internet media, the performance of failure as a solicitation of laughter, and the ironic stance of certain forms of contemporary spectatorship.

## Failing in Public

As discussed earlier, the performance of character types is a well-worn tradition in comedic performance. In Japanese variety television this is usually organized by the *boke* and *tsukkomi* roles from *manzai* comedy. This section will highlight some of the ways these concepts appear on Niconico through both the commenting by audiences and through the performances of video uploaders. The way commenting audiences enact a variation on *tsukkomi*-style mocking humor has already been discussed, but it is also worth touching on how the players and streamers take up roles within familiar frames. These general roles in commonly understood and widely circulated patterns of humor are performed in addition to the character or role specific to a particular video. This has previously been discussed in terms of ambivalence or ugliness in performance and media practice, particularly through how the relationship between the player and the commenting spectator is enacted as a semi-reciprocal meta-interaction in which they play off of one another's routines. As with the preceding section, this will be related to recent developments in television comedy, but we will also try to identify what is salient about performances specifically on Niconico and the type of ambivalence they invoke.

Failing at games during a video or stream is one area where this circulation of performance is frequently enacted. Previous examples such as the Metal Gear Solid 4 playthrough and P-P's sessions of Super Mario Brothers with a DDR pad fit into this mold. But it isn't just the prevalence of audience *tsukkomi*-style comments by which these videos demonstrate the circulation of comedic performance. It is also the players' *boke*-like ability to fail that is used to solicit laughter from an audience, particularly one that can recognize those patterns and produce the appropriate reaction. In other words, the performance of failure before an audience is one that imagines a kind of public that can react to the player's performance and participate in the circuit of laughter.

This kind of solicitation of *tsukkomi*-style commenting is one of the major qualities of "let's play" videos' mode of participation and comedic exchange. The spectators watching and responding in the comment feed assume the same kind of stance as the comedians watching on the monitor of *TV that Will Make You Laugh*, based on a similar understanding of being in on the joke through the way they experience the video as watching and commenting together. This is also where we might find the ugliness of these videos and the ambivalent qualities of the performance types that circulate between players and audiences. However, the big difference between these videos and variety television is that the video uploader is also in on the joke through his or her assumption of a *boke* stance of soliciting ironic comments via a performance of failing in public. This forms the semi-reciprocal element of these kinds of performances. In other words, it is this fitting into a pattern or network of roles and positions in a more abstract circuit of meta-interaction that produces this sense of game-becoming, ambivalent laughter.

What, then, is the agency of failure in these types of videos? On the one hand the foregrounding of *boke* performances in "let's play" videos as a way of initiating audiences' sense of being in on the joke and laughing at the performer's failure is another form of ugly ambivalence expressed in these videos. It decenters the economy of performance that is presupposed by the *manzai* model, in which different users or performers fit into different roles that interact in symmetrical ways. Although the *tsukkomi* vision of the audience or panel assumes an asymmetrical knowledge of the situation, compared to the unknowing *boke*, the distribution of those roles suggests a reciprocal mode of performance. In the case of "let's play" videos, it is actually the player who is soliciting the *tsukkomi*-style comments from the audience that will make fun of him or her. The degree to which this laughter can be described as being at the expense of the player seems less certain now. The audience may laugh as if at the expense of the player, but that is actually part of the circuit of laughter initiated by the model of performance taken up by the player. This shift in asymmetry between users is then another form of ambivalence that informs how these videos are made and watched.

This sense of ambivalence can also be extended to how similar performances on variety television function. Although presented as documentary images of unsuspecting failure or humiliation, variety shows that feature pranks, comedic traps, or outlandish setups are also typically rigged so that the *boke* performer is aware of the routine even as he or she is being laughed at. This can be done for safety concerns, but the general reason is to ensure a good reaction from the *boke*, who, being in on the joke, can prepare to react in an entertaining way. There is even a category for this type of performer in variety television who plays at being caught off guard: "reaction artist" (*riakushion geinin*).

What is the ultimate significance of being in on the joke in this type of media? Does the performer's being in the joke extend to how the routine is being imagined? Images of failure remain important to "let's play" videos and other types of game-related visual media, and, indeed, the attraction for the audience (through an understanding of the genre or particular program or player) is the expectation of seeing a spectacularized moment of failure that can be laughed at. There is perhaps a sense of affirmation that comes with this. In being able to laugh at someone or something, audiences can maintain a pseudo-superior position to that which they are watching. But the strong ambivalence of this type of media and its characteristics of ugliness must also be acknowledged. The solicitation of a particular way of viewing and laughing is compounded by the seemingly endless rewriting of the media itself, decentering the mode of authorship away from the original video maker and player just as the mode of performance disrupts assumedly symmetrical roles or types that audiences and performers fall into. The "in-betweenness" of the media form that is constantly between different types of practice is thus counterbalanced by a type of laughter that is between different ways of imagining the social experience of online, meta-interactive visual culture.

# POSTSCRIPT
Out of Time

On August 16, 2012, Niconico opened a promotional tent at Fuji Television's United States of Odaiba event. The tent was operated by staff who showed visitors around, introduced them to the event's theme (a tropical island paradise), and offered prizes for attendees who participated in the festivities. The chief attraction was the "Nico Shrine" (*Nico jinja*), a large monitor with a camera attached to it that visitors were invited to approach to make a wish to the "gods" (*kamisama*) of Niconico. These gods were in fact the anonymous audience watching a video stream of the shrine online who could see and hear the visitors. Assuming this role of the "gods" of the shrine, online users could write responses to their requests in the comment feed, which were then shown on the screen live at the site in Odaiba. The idea was that visitors would ask for something such as doing well in school or having things go well with a significant other, and then the online commentators would respond "okay" to approve their wish. Families and couples visited the shrine in small groups, made their requests, waited for a response, and then moved on to the next part of the exhibit after receiving a response to their wish. The rapport between the live visitors and the online "gods" was friendly, with online users granting all wishes and even complimenting the visitors on their appearance or sense of style and offering encouragement in their studies and work.

One exchange between the live attendees and the online audience stands out. Among the many guests who visited the shrine were a father and his two elementary-school-aged sons. This family of three wasn't familiar with Niconico but was guided through the shrine by one of the staff members, who showed the boys how to speak to the online wish-granters while their father suggested things they might ask for. Messages scrolled across the screen as the family was figuring out what to say—"Your dad's handsome" (*papa ikemen*) and "nice bandana" were among the many greetings that appeared onscreen. While figuring out what to wish for, one of the boys remarked that he was hungry, which led his father to ask if he wanted to eat tuna sushi. Within a few moments an intricate comment art representation of a piece of sushi scrolled across the screen, drawing cheers from the other online audience members, who praised the comment artist for the skill and speed in delivering the visitor's wish.

However, by the time the comment art scrolled across the screen of the shrine, the two boys had already turned away. The impressive display had gone unseen by its intended audience. The futility of the comment artist's efforts brought waves of laughter from the other online viewers, who jokingly responded "they weren't watching, lolol" (*mite nai wwww*). The staff member asked the comment artist to make another piece of art for the children (with the other online viewers cheering him or her on as well), but the boys had moved on to another exhibit by the time the second piece of comment art was complete and displayed on the shrine's monitor.

This book began with an example of an online audience watching a live event on Niconico and streaming media sites such as UStream. In that case the anonymous audience turned on their would-be allies who were protesting in person, laughing at the way the anti-Korean demonstrators blended into crowds of meandering tourists visiting the TV station campus. The related example just described, of visitors to the same annual event a year later, can help revise some of this book's ideas about online sociality and media culture. This case is in many ways the opposite of the one described in the introduction. The online audience is friendly rather than hostile, and it is the "live" attendees who transform the event into unintentional comedy by not watching. In both cases the live visitors are unaware in different ways, but the online audience in the second case exhibits sincerity rather than cynical elitism.

In the first example I emphasized the self-presentation of laughter among online audiences and the technologically mediated social forms they engaged with over the actual-world nationalism of protesters at that event. For this bookend I focus on how the "out of joint" timing of the online commenters and the live attendees produced a missed connection—the two boys' failure to see the comment art. The brief delay between what online users type and what the live attendees see, and the time it takes to prepare comment art, undermines the shrine's intent to offer live interaction between the unseen, anonymous users online and the tourists shown on camera. The asymmetricality in representation compounds the asynchronicity of the media interface, resulting in timing that is off just enough so that the hard work by comment artists goes unnoticed, turning an intended moment of triumph into a moment of laughter at this how this gesture went awry. The audience laughs at the ambivalent behavior of the two children, but it is also laughing at itself—the "gods" of the shrine—for being made powerless.

These examples, above and in the introduction, demonstrate many of the ideas introduced in this book, including the slippery sociality of online anonymity, the representational problems of asynchronous experiences of time, and the interstitial layering in aesthetics that grows out of technological mediation. We can also see a refrain of how laughter and play fit into online sociality and how anonymous users act in aggregate through textual modes of representation. This is not the same thing as acting in unison, but it also points toward a deindividualized mode of conduct centered on patterns of repetition that grant the appearance and feeling of coordination and spontaneity at the same time.

This conclusion will focus on the experience of time in the case described above. The brief gap in time between the online audience responding and the live attendees being present renders this as a moment of asynchronicity, but it is not the same kind of asynchronicity as the pseudo-synchronicity of Niconico's comment feed or the selective-synchronicity of Twitter's messaging system (Hamano 2008a). This brief, barely noticeable gap is what we might describe as "plesiochronicity." This is a kind of time that is almost synchronic but off just enough to render things "out of joint." K. J. Donnelly uses this term to describe the aesthetics of film sound synchronization, such as in crowd and street scenes that rely on a general sound that seems could be emanating from what we see but is actually not linked to any particular source or series of sources (Donnelly 2013, 182). Donnelly connects this to the feeling of sound and image "drifting apart," in which multiple tracks appear to almost line up but are set to slightly different clocks that allow for a feeling of disconnection. This can result in an uncanny aesthetic in which our senses discern that something is slightly off, but it also points to the way mechanical recording and technological transmission of visual and auditory information are often just barely out of sync.

The sense of plesiochronicity and just barely being out of step is something we can perceive in a variety of live online media, such as video streaming and online gaming. Some of these cases have been discussed earlier. Latency in online games can cause another player's character to appear ahead of or behind the space it should actually be represented as occupying, and delays in voice-chat and video feeds cause conversations to hiccup and pause, leading to participants accidently speaking over one another. Liveness as a category of experience in online media and its rhetoric and connectivity should therefore be revised to consider how the types of connection offered by these media are frequently interrupted by a sense of drifting apart or a gap in time between users. This is especially relevant in terms of how online media work in reference to actual-world events and social forms, and the ambivalent dimension that emerges in that relationship. In keeping with this book's focus on the ways social disconnection can be recovered as connection, in plesiochronic media we need to attend to the ways users learn to navigate such gaps and fissures in time and develop ways of watching, playing, and communicating around the inherent latency and structured delays in online media.

Twitch.tv (the video streaming site specializing in video game playthroughs discussed in chapter 5) offers another example in approaching how slightly off registers of time result in an experience of disconnection. The timing between the chat window audiences use to follow along and communicate with the player (and each other) and the main video window, which shows the streamer's content, is typically off by a few seconds. In most cases this delay lasts around five seconds, but users sometimes experience latency as prolonged as twenty or even thirty seconds. Although many streamers run their channels like an informal chat with the audience, this gap in time between what they say, the time the audience hears it, and the time the audience's response can be seen by them disrupts a feeling of smooth, uninterrupted liveness. The flow of conversation is instead halting and awkward, with the streamer often having to wait to see the written responses of users in the chat window.

To return to the idea of watching and playing as if together, this slight delay in time results in moments of interruption as the audience watching along witnesses an on-camera event seconds after it has already concluded. This means that when the player pulls off an impressive feat—such as in an elite challenge attempt in a fast-paced game such as Dustforce (Hitbox 2012)—the audience will only see it after it has happened. Their written reactions of surprise and praise will therefore only be entered and made visible to the player after a noticeable gap in time has passed. This means that comments congratulating the player on a task well done will appear after that moment has passed and even sometimes humorously appear to comment on moments of failure as they player restarts the game for a new run or session.

The sense of liveness is thus one that cannot address itself simultaneously, foregrounding the qualification of "as if" in a very specific way. For the audience, what they see appears to be happening live, but the streamer's experience is one of delay, in which the text chat is constantly falling behind. This is also highly pronounced in livestreams that feature multiple players communicating with one another through a voice-chat program such as Discord, which allows them to speak with "live" simultaneity even though their ability to watch the images of the video stream are delayed through the site's inherent latency. Reactions to what happens on camera are thus delayed, resulting in the player experiencing something before anyone else can see what is happening, causing them to listen to his or her reactions while having the images withheld. This often causes the player to wait for the reactions of other viewers for a few seconds after a moment of success or failure in order to share their own reactions in animated ways.

The quality of watching or playing together in these cases happens through the reciprocity of reactions. The interface of the site forces users to deal with a lag in time between what different users can see and communicate, shifting the experience of "together" away from live simultaneity (which is not actually possible) to practices of waiting for others to catch up in order to indulge in their displays of shock, laughter, and appreciation. In other words, while the quality of time that Twitch.tv allows for interrupts users' ability to share in simultaneous experiences, users adapt and recenter the impulse to share experiences immediately and adjust to the interval of lag and interruption. The impossibility of literal simultaneity in experience is therefore relieved by a practice of "as if" watching or playing together, one that adapts the indifference of the technological interface of the site to more cordial practices of waiting. We again have a mix of pseudo-coordination and spontaneity to produce an interstitial experience of "as if" togetherness. This constitutes another form of social interaction that is mediated by commercial media architecture and design.

A curious reversal of this dynamic of delay can be found in user-input-driven game emulation channels hosted on Twitch.tv, such as Twitch Plays Pokemon. This channel, which uses an emulator to host crowd-sourced playthroughs of Pokemon video games, uses chat-bot programs to read and translate user commands entered in the chat to direct the in-game actions. This includes moving the character around the screen, selecting items, and managing options in combat. There is no player or streamer actively running the channel, only the chat-bot program that understands certain commands entered by the audience (directional commands as well as "A," "B," "start," and "select") that are then translated into input commands for the playerless game. This is perhaps the most literal attempt at putting "let's play" into "let's play"–style video making and streaming in that an individual player is removed in favor of transforming the audience into a community of players. But there are elements of delay and an aggregation of commands that should be addressed.

When the Twitch Plays Pokemon channel began in February 2014, commands entered into the chat were read directly into the game. However, because tens of thousands of users would be watching and entering commands at any given time, the sheer volume of input caused a chaotic sense of un-coordination as a backlog of commands piled up while the game was still processing those made earlier. The system couldn't keep up with the rate at which the audience was adding new commands. Users tried to issue commands based on the present game state they were seeing onscreen, believing their input would be read and carried out immediately. But because of the backlog there was a delay that caused commands to be read and carried out seconds after they were intended. As such, commands frequently did not address the present game state and led to loops of ineffective action, causing the game to run off the rails repeatedly.

To correct this, a system of translating individual command inputs into votes for a single command drawn out of the aggregate was introduced. This meta-command was designed to read user-made input periodically, slowing the pace of the game but also streamlining it to act more like a coordinated intelligence was guiding it. This led to some users trying to deliberately input wrong commands and throw off the path to success, a practice that became a game within the game for these "trolls." This too was eventually incorporated into the chat-script, allowing players to vote for two opposing game states. The first, "democracy," was a game state in which input commands were averaged and required a large majority of participants to enter the same commands. The second, "anarchy," was a game state in which commands were needed to direct the game toward a single action. But based on what game state the users were voting for at a given time, the types of commands that could influence the game state varied and disrupted the appearance of coordination in unpredictable ways.

The delay between the time of input of a command and the time it was actually read into the game's commands began to transform through these changes in how the channel's chat-bots read the audience's input commands. The immediate, chaotic sense of uncontrollability of the channel's initial version gave way to a slower, more coordinated sense of vote-based gaming that drew on aggregate commands and streamlined the number of inputs being fed to the game. Up to thirty seconds would pass between the time of input of a command into the chat and the time it would (or wouldn't) be factored into the onscreen actions in the game. As such, the experience of immediacy—which was messy and unpredictable—was phased out in favor of one that could more readily allow the users to progress through the game. It took users of the channel two weeks to clear the first game in the series, Pokemon Red, paving the way for more recent installments in the series to be played via emulation and aggregate input commands. The channel also inspired many other "twitch play" channels that used chat to control the character in other types of games, such as the puzzle game Tetris and even competitive fighting games such as Street Fighter II.

The intensification of near-simultaneous media and communication described in the previous examples (and throughout this book) can also be contextualized within wider concerns about how human relationships have transformed in response to computer-mediated communication. Name-attributed social media use in Japan is sometimes characterized in terms of "fatigue" due to the expectations of replying to people one might know at work and at school, adding users known in actual-life social networks to one's online circle, and an overall feeling of obligation that comes through maintaining a kind of online portfolio that mirrors or compliments offline existence. This has been particularly severe in cases such as the pressure to accept friend requests, comment on posts, and "like" messages from superiors at work or seniors at school in sites such as Mixi and Facebook. This general sense of frustration with social media has been characterized as "Mixi fatigue" (*mixi tsukare*) to account for the sense of exhaustion stemming from qualities of social maintenance and obligation that are sustained and rehearsed through such media (Hamano and Sasaki 2011, 106). A related issue can be found in the demand of replying to mobile phone texting—which in some social environments is expected to be done right away, even to the point where users will mass-message their contacts a warning message when going through an area without service such as a tunnel. What emerges is a sense that maintaining social relationships through online media has become excessively demanding and psychically exhausting.

Online media that eschew recognizable usernames, persistent accounts, or recognizable links to actual-world identities offer a relief to these issues of fatigue, but they also usher in a more generally relaxed form of sociality. Some critics and journalists writing on media such as 2channel have suggested that the difficulty of addressing someone you don't know can be lifted by the casual atmosphere of online anonymity, which often uses very informal language and no recognizable social hierarchy for users to obey. In one sense this helps create a sense of "carnivalesque" social relations, but it also contributes to the type of language and language ideology that online communities engage in.[1] As one example, we can look at the previously discussed tendency toward laddish, masculine-coded language in anonymous media, such as in how messages posted to 2channel or the Niconico comment feed frequently use the communal personal pronoun *ore* and, when addressing the group, refer to other users as *omaera*. The use of "dialect cosplay" described in chapter 3 represents another case of language used in screen-based communication in which the individual users are unseen. One the one hand, these contribute to the sense of freeing users from their actual-world identities and networks of social conduct and directs them toward participating in the aggregate cultural identity of the site. This can be an attractive alternative to actual-world sociality for some. However, it also risks universalizing that style of identity (masculine, informal) for all users by creating an impression of naturalized address and encoding self-presentation through language selection. In that sense, while the forms of connectivity offered by these media might offer relief from the social atomization felt by many in post-recession Japan, that severance from actual-world sociality and identities can also turn into a form of disavowal that we can associate with the neoliberal championing of the individual at the expense of a more socially committed way of being.

These cases bespeak larger concerns about asymmetricality raised in this book and the media forms it has analyzed. The opening episode of the protesters outside of Fuji TV's Odaiba campus demonstrated asymmetrical modes of representation and participation between in-person attendees and online audiences, while media like Niconico's shrine and Twitch.tv's inherent lag present asymmetricality in how visual information is displayed to different audiences, who experience the same media through a plesiochronic representation of time that places different users in registers of time that are slightly off. In the latter settings, communication seems as though it will be live and simultaneous, but minute differences in time between users constantly interrupt the flow of their experiences. The gaps time hinder their ability to communicate smoothly, but they also thwart the possibility of engaging in symmetrical play and exchange.

This asymmetricality in representation, which is part of a general move toward the aggregate instead of the individual in networked media, is compounded by the ways that these users are constantly behind in time in relation to the performers or other users they are watching, being watched by, and communicating with. They see things happen after the fact, and their reactions can only be seen when it is too late, leading to moments of confusion, interruption, and waiting. For the impatient party (such as the two young boys in the Nico shrine example) this can mean disconnection. But in settings of cooperation, such as playing as if together, users might wait for one another and be able to laugh alongside each other at the same thing. In this sense, anonymous audiences are marked, not necessarily in terms of legible identity but in being "out of time" and constantly falling behind other kinds of users.

These experiences of being "out of time" resonate with the visual aesthetic of opacity in the media forms described throughout this book. The gaps in experience and comprehension that open and interrupt the way we use media organize how new media practices and routines appear, adding to the ways that different cultures of use emerge and how communities organized around online media learn to communicate with one another. They also change how we look at these media, often interpreting multiple layers of information at the same time and visually folding back one layer to concentrate on another. This book is rapidly reaching its conclusion—another form of being "out of time"—but I hope this final contemplation of how media interfaces contribute to how the experiences of time, space, and the social walk a balance between connection and disconnection and recover interaction between users through these interruptions. Being out of time is not just the experience of being too late, off center, or off the mark but also a space of opening up different forms of communication through the abstractions of technological mediation. This newness is also part of how these media fit into the contemporary social landscape in and around Japan, such as how they provide alternative ways of organizing social relations and mediating the individual with the aggregate.

As one aspect of contemporary media culture, these qualities of interstitiality might then also be viewed not just as something that separates but as something that fills in, that makes media experiences feel more complete or more connected even as they are drifting apart. The different forms of online media discussed in this book—video commenting systems, repetitive posting driven by automated deletion, and livestreaming commentary—contribute to this visual syntax of barrage and its capacity to overwhelm, distract, and produce feelings of connection through their mediation of time and representation. The visual and cultural dimensions of barrage are therefore not just questions of media aesthetics but also part of the logic through which users learn to interact through and around the technological interfaces of the media they watch, write, and play with.

# Notes

**INTRODUCTION**

1. Marc Steinberg connects online reactionary political movements and expressions on sites such as 2channel to a more general reactionary "swing" of political energy in contemporary Japan. Steinberg 2019, 194.

2. Takaoka's status as celebrity martyr for the anti-Korean online movement went through many transformations in the immediate wake of his initial Twitter outburst. His contract with the entertainment agency Stardust Promotion was nullified on July 28. This led to an outpouring of sympathy for his position and further outrage against Fuji TV. Such sentiments overlapped with rumors of Koreans working in the upper echelons of the entertainment industry of Japan (a longstanding suspicion of anti-Fuji crusaders) as part of a conspiracy to silence any kind of anti-Korean sentiment in public discourse. The manner in which the story and Takaoka's personal involvement was covered on news programs—including those on Fuji—also led to further agitation about perceived biases against anti-Korean and right-wing nationalist online activists (often called *netto uyoku* or *netto-uyo*). However, over time Takaoka's participation in programs that were perceived to be part of Fuji TV's promotion of Korean media in Japan became more widely discussed. This in turn caused many to abandon him as a rallying point for the political goals of the movement.

3. The protests were originally scheduled for August 8 and used the hashtag #nofuji88 to promote the event on Twitter. Fuji TV is channel 8 in Japan, so August 8 was chosen to capitalize on the numerical connection. However, because Fuji was planning on holding a special event that day, the actual day of the protest was changed. A similar event was held on August 21. And although Fuji TV—along with the *Asahi Shinbun*—has long been one of the favorite targets for online nationalists in Japan, there is a certain irony to this. As Yasuda Koichi (2012) notes, Fuji Television initially styled itself as a lone conservative voice amid the tide of liberal mass media in Japan. The network's use of licensed content from South Korea to cut production costs damaged this image for some on the political right in Japan and helped lead to the impression among some online users that the network was allying itself with South Korea or even coming under the sway of powerful Koreans living in Japan.

4. Kitada Akihiro (2005) has made this connection between online anonymity and elitism, writing specifically about the message board 2channel and the development of what he describes as "cynical nationalism."

5. Sianne Ngai has written about the "ugly feelings" of aesthetic life under capitalism, connecting emotion to questions of personal agency and the over-administered quality of modern life. Ngai 2007, 1.

6. Paul Roquet (2016) has noted the intersection of the desire for an unmarked identity with fantasies of personal autonomy and freedom from social responsibility.

7. These social problems have been written about widely in journalistic and academic venues alike. For a summary of issues such as *hikikomori*, overworked populations, and school bullying, see Cwiertka and Machotka, 2018.

8. The language of "in joke" (*uchiwa*) is also borrowed from Kitada, who uses this term as part of his explanation of the elitist tendencies of 2channel. In jokes become part of the

rhetoric of border patrolling, rendering outsiders as having a deficit of knowledge that prevents them from engaging. Kitada 2005, 11–13.

9. The personalities of so-called Weird Twitter provide one example of this. John Herman and Katie Notopoulos have interviewed some of these (some while in character). See Herman and Notopulus 2013.

10. Laura Marks describes ASCII art as "community-based" due to its circulation among users and its amateur status. She also links this to a nostalgia for "cruder" computer interfaces, describing it as a "political refusal of the upgrade trap." The "low" aesthetics of ASCII art and its reproducibility via copying and pasting intersect with a more general aesthetics of incompleteness of internet culture and other parts of contemporary media in Japan. Marks 2002, 181–83.

11. Boellstorff 2008, 151.

12. This term and "selective synchronicity" are translations of Hamano Satoshi's terms *giji-dōki* and *sentaku-dōki*. Both of these will be discussed later on in reference to Hamano's work.

13. Zheng 2016, 323, 324. Zheng's research is focused primarily on Chinese-language versions of barrage-style video media, but she also maintains a comparative approach that traces language used in fan and *otaku*-style subcultures to Japanese counterparts.

14. The popularity of internet cafes and PC bangs (their South Korean equivalent) is another part of internet culture in East Asia that can be distinguished from those in the West. These intersect with local gaming cultures and the availability of high-powered computers and internet connections.

15. Olga Fedorenko (2014) describes television advertising in South Korea this way, characterizing it both as a form of popular culture and a site of melodrama.

16. As Galloway writes, "software is an example of technical transcoding without figuration that nevertheless coexists with an exceedingly high level of ideological fetishism and misrecognition." He goes on to say that this is "the very definition of ideology." Galloway 2006, 319.

17. Galloway is drawing on Wendy Chun's assertion: "What is software if not the very effort of making something explicit, or making something intangible visible, while at the same time rendering the visible (such as the machine) invisible?" Chun 2005, 44.

18. Nozawa 2012.

19. The expression "to-be-looked-at-ness" comes from Laura Mulvey's well-known essay on the male gaze in Hollywood cinema, "Visual Pleasure and Narrative Cinema." Mulvey 1975.

20. For more on time-shifting media, see Cubitt 1991.

21. Mary Anne Doane's *The Emergence of Cinematic Time* offers an account of how photography, travel, and related forms of modern culture contributed to time as an issue of representation in everyday life.

22. Laura Marks aligns her project on Islamic art's affinity with new media as engaging with the "ignored underside of history," which she characterizes as discontinuity due to the way she breaks from more conventional narratives of the historical development of art, science, and technology. Ambivalently dealing with media culture from Japan is obviously not the same thing as advocating for a historical reevaluation of the place of Islamic art and technology in Western academic understandings of history, especially at the present, but this book (*Textual Cacophony*) aspires to a related practice of introducing "area"-marked materials into media studies scholarship. Marks 2010, 25.

23. Marc Steinberg notes the role Japanese media and technology have played in developing the theory and practice of what he describes as "platforms," which he positions as an alternative to the network as a defining part of contemporary media culture. This notion of the platform extends to issues of economics and management in media properties

and services, and also to Japan's development of mobile-based internet infrastructures, as contrasted with a computer-based internet. See Steinberg 2019, 3, 7.

24. Iwabuchi Koichi (2002) has famously described globalization and popular culture as a process of "recentering" within regional structures where Japan acts as an interpreter or interface between the United States and East Asia more broadly.

25. 4chan summary sites such as warosu.org also riff on this affinity with Japan, both through the name of the site (*warosu* is a corruption of the Japanese verb for "to laugh," *warau*) and the content focus on Japan-themed threads.

26. Some Vaporwave artists even title their songs and albums and convey their performance handles in Japanese text. See Tanner (2016) for more on this type of music and visual culture.

27. For more on the changing of the guard at 2channel, see Akimoto 2014. Steinberg (2017) also discusses the merger between Kadokawa and Dwango.

## 1. ANIMATED WRITING

1. Donald Crafton (2012) has written extensively on this topic in relation to American cartoon animation.

2. For a summary of these arguments, see Apter 2005, 228.

3. Alexandra Jaffe discusses this type of process in relation to how language is used in mainstream media. Jaffe 2011, 567.

4. Jaffe and Shan Walton have connected non-standard orthography to speech, focusing on the "reading performances" of vocalized text. Jaffe and Walton 2000.

5. In 2016 Niconico had the ninth-highest number of daily visitors in Japan according to the web traffic research company Alexa. Sites that ranked higher than Niconico included Yahoo.jp, Google.co.jp, FC2 (a video-sharing site discussed in chapter 3), and Twitter.

6. Jinying Li notes that *danmaku* media in Chinese-language settings are called *danmu* and that this term usually refers to the entire interface of the media display, rather than just the comments. Li 2017, 235n2.

7. For more on Miku and Vocaloid videos and their popularity on Niconico, see Tomita Akihiro 2008, 24–29. For an introduction to the discourse of *naka no hito* (the person inside), see Ishida 2008.

8. For more on these Chinese-language sites, see Zheng 2017.

9. Natsuno Takeshi, an assistant executive at the company the manages Niconico places the ratio at 63 percent. Natsuno 2011.

10. The site also introduced a wiki-style encyclopedia of user-made entries, which can be viewed as part of Niconico's persistent anchoring in net culture despite its shift toward mainstream and commercial media. Steinberg 2017 92, 93.

11. This aesthetic bears some resemblance to the way that cel animation sometimes appears. The spatial dynamic of cel animation is often organized around two layers the plane on which the figures move and the plane they appear to move through as part of their constructed, diegetic world. In the case of Niconico, the layering of the comments over the video image produces a sense of near-integration between the two planes but also preserves the inconsistency in how they move, the quality of detail in which they appear, et cetera. For more on layering spaces in cel animation, see Crafton 2012.

12. This style of commenting was also originally made available for videos uploaded to Youtube, which could then be watched using Niconico's interface, but this was shut down by Youtube. See Kanose 2010, 71.

13. Hamano 2008a, 197. Hamano elaborates on his research on internet communication in an interview with Azuma Hiroki. Hamano and Hiroki 2012, 144–209.

14. See Nozawa 2012 for more on pseudo-anonymous communication and performance in Japan, Niconico in particular. For more on crowds, mimesis, and affect, see Mazzarella 2010, 697–727.

15. Fukushima Ryōta has also drawn attention to the important role that time plays in internet communication and in organizing the modes of experience in online environments. He questions that emphasis on "space" (*kukan*) and feelings of proximity that other writers have made in pursuing similar topics, arguing that a feeling of time is how users "match" with one another in creating a sense of shared experience. Fukushima 2010, 13–14.

16. Bakhtin 1984, 14. My reading of Bakhtin's notion of the polyphonic is indebted to Naoki Sakai's use of the term, particularly his gloss that the polyphonic allows the reader to become a "participant." Sakai 1992, 26.

17. Nishimura 2003, 338.

18. Azuma 2011. See also the English-language translation by John Person (Azuma 2014).

19. Azuma 2011 (Azuma 2014, 95).

20. Azuma 2011, 84 (Azuma 2014, 56). From an inverse perspective, Google's Japanese IME was initially released with an archive of terms and phrases taken from popular culture such as television animation. It would therefore suggest famous quotes or lines of dialogue as part of the autocomplete function.

21. Mistakes made by autocorrect software in mobile texting perhaps come closer to actually disrupting the agency of the human user. Jeff Scheible discusses autocorrect failures in relation to efficiency and collaborative writing. Scheible 2015, 23.

22. Phillips 2016, 56.

23. Azuma 2011, 126 (Azuma 2014, 92–93).

24. Hamano 2008b.

25. Inoue 2006, 130

26. *Hachi* can also be read as *pachi* in some circumstances through the *handakuten* diacritic, a small circle that indicates that a syllable starting with 'h' should instead be pronounced as beginning with 'p'

27. For some examples of the use of foreign alphabets in mobile phone texting, see L. Miller 2004, 225–47.

28. Uchiyama 2010 gives an overview of some of the wordplay in typography used on 2channel and Niconico. Murakami Naomichi and Ito Eisuke similarly document some of the ways language is used on music-related internet videos in two essays published in 2010 and 2011.

29. Tsunda Daisuke notes the "loose" quality of discourse on social media such as Twitter in which strangers address one another in familiar ways. He characterizes this as part of the site's feeling of "directness" in communication. As with Niconico, this coincides with the way the site represents time, which Hamano describes as "selective synchronicity" but Tsunda equates with a new sense of "real time" that discards moments of "dead time" between interactions to produce a feeling of constant activity. The ways online media represent time in ways that encode directness can therefore be linked to the familiar, casual ways in which anonymous users address and interact with one another. Tsunda 2009, 51.

30. In Japanese this is usually called *boinyugo* but is also sometimes more informally described as *edokokei*, referring to its association with residents of old Tokyo (and the Shitamachi area in particular). For more on vowel coalescence in Japanese, see Inada 2008.

31. Matsuda 2006. Sites that summarize popular threads from 2channel (*matome*) will sometimes use different colors and font sizes to emphasize well-received posts.

## 2. CHARACTERS OF LANGUAGE

1. See Nozawa 2014 for more on the idea of *kyara* in Japanese media and the possibilities of "living as a character."

2. Writing over someone else's work is not always considered legitimate, but it does play into structures of recognition, one-upping, and local prestige. See, for example, Felisbret 2009, 88.

3. David Rodowick's observation that certain kinds of figural text-images disrupt the way that looking and reading are typically rendered as separate activities points toward a similar way that some kinds of text require different techniques of reading. Rodowick 2001, 62, 63.

4. This video is essentially just an audio track featuring a medley of some songs famous on Niconico and an automated background design created by a music player program such as Winamp or Windows Media Player. There are a few such videos on the site, some of which are used for innovative comment art such as the kind described here.

5. The song used in this particular video is a MIDI version, so there is no vocal track. The aligning of the comments with the song is something that is being "remembered" by both the commenters and those watching the video. This is another way of considering the practices of animation that Niconico users engage in.

6. This is a gloss on Silvio's summary of these concepts. Most work on animation as a kind of movement of images adopts a more concrete definition, but I find Silvio's abstraction of animation to a kind of environmental vision and sense of relationality to be very insightful.

7. Another variation of this is a Japanese IME offered by Google, which, as described previously, will sometimes make "suggestions" to the user via the drop-down menu by drawing on famous quotes from anime or other popular media. This kind of joking "anticipation" of what the user will write might be seen as animating the process of typing similar to the way that Marks describes the changing typography in Arabic fonts, in the sense that the computer seems to be performing some kind of activity in anticipation of what the operator is doing.

8. In this case *ne* is a slang version of *nai*. The changing of *nai* into *ne* in negative verbs and adjectives is a common form of vowel coalescence in spoken Japanese.

9. The use of romanized Greek first appeared as a solution to the lack of support for Greek characters in early ASCII, but so-called Greeklish has persisted even though Greek-friendly IMEs have appeared. Tseliga 2007, 135.

## 3. REPERTOIRE AND ACCUMULATION

1. I am borrowing this phrase from Apter 2005, 223.

2. Taylor 2003, xix. Taylor characterizes this dynamic as archives assuming a kind of endurance through their material existence, and performance (repertoire) offering a way of transforming the ephemeral into something lasting. Taylor 2003, 19.

3. This not to suggest that these other forms of writing are permanent but rather to foreground the qualities of inherent impermanence and immateriality in online writing and archiving.

4. Yanagita 2010, 167–202.

5. We can find related examples on online happenings in non-Japanese media as well. Both Whitney Phillips and Gabriella Coleman have written on virtual "raids" of online social and game spaces, such as when the Habbo Hotel social media platform was invaded by users from Something Awful and 4chan. While obviously orchestrated to some extent, these events also display qualities of loose association between their participants,

a carnivalesque disruption of social spaces, and temporalities of abruptness. See Phillips 2016, 129–30; and Coleman 2014, 45–46.

6. For his analysis of 2channel postings in the wake of 9/11, see Suzuki 2002, 30–31. For his writing on the reaction to the return of the Japanese hostages from Iraq, see Suzuki 2006, 5–7. For more on the intersection between online media and emerging regimes of belief, suspicion, and trust in news reportage, see Tomabechi 2011.

7. Suzuki points toward things such as copy-and-paste posting, ASCII art, and blocks of preformatted text as signs of this move away from "content" in trolling. Suzuki 2002, 180.

8. This sense of apolitical participation is, of course, encoded with a particular kind of politics. This can be compared to the way that some critics have written about nationalistic discourse online and the "normality" of the people who engage in this kind of behavior. See, for example, Yasuda Koichi 2012 on anti-Korean internet activism in Japan.

9. Hamano 2008a, 238. The idea of "invasion" is also tied to the tendency of users of 2channel to target other websites (such as Mixi) or the mass media in their pranking and harassment.

10. Referring to how the comment feed of a video might appear at any given time as a "version" is problematic in that it would seem to assume a clear beginning and end of different feeds. The feed is more accurately approached as a single media object that transforms over time and shifts gradually rather than having distinct beginning or end points for any single "version." However, for the purposes of describing the way these transformations are felt between different instances of use (time elapses between visits, etc.), describing the feed as a series of semi-discrete instances can help clarify the degree to which this transformation is visible.

11. See, for example, Saether 2010.

12. The use of hashtags (messages accompanied by the symbol #) on English-language social media sites present an adjacent phenomenon. By linking individual messages through shared language and content, sites such as Twitter intensify the temporal aspects of internet writing while also deindividualizing instances of use by transforming them into part of an evolving archive of connected content. As Jeff Scheible notes, this organization of messages dilutes the authority of individual users and positions, instead transforming them into the network logic of "trending" topics that are tied to the moment-to-moment accumulation of text. The grouping of messages using similar language and posted in temporal proximity through trending topics and hashtags also allows individual instances to become part of an archive of immediacy, and journalists writing for online news media have frequently used messages posted to Twitter to provide quotations and reactions from celebrities and ordinary users alike. This is different from a thread on 2channel or the comment feed of a video on Niconico, of course, in that users are not necessarily posting on the same page, "wall," or media object but rather having their messages collected through the pseudo-archiving features of the site itself. Still, both speak to ways in which online media modify (and intensify) the temporal aspects of individual acts of writing by tying them to other instances of use through an archive-like logic of accumulation. See Scheible 2015, 111.

13. Phillips draws on Christie Davies's work on mass media coverage of disasters to analyze the relationship between trolls in English-language internet media (particularly 4chan) and the theatricalization of such events in television news, noting that the spatial, temporal, and geographic mediation of televised tragedies allows for (and even makes necessary) some form of emotional detachment or comedic response. Phillips 2016, 116.

14. Butler 1993, 12, 24n7. Repetition is also addressed in *Gender Trouble*, where Butler considers the role of repetition in performance as a kind of legitimization before a public. Butler 1990, 140.

15. Butler 1993, 25n7. Here Butler is building on Derrida's notion of "iterability" (Derrida 1977).

## 4. COLLECTING, COPYING, AND COPYRIGHT

1. Hamano Satoshi and Kobayashi Hiroto discuss sharing as a concept in need of requalification in online media in their interview conversation. Hamano and Kobayashi 2010, 51–52. Kobayashi elaborates on the relationship between sharing (as an economic and cultural practices) and online sociality in his book *Shiea* (Share) (2010).

2. Much has been written about media convergence in Japan and East Asia more broadly, and also more generally as an aspect of contemporary media platforms and the intersection of production, consumption, and culture. For Japan-specific cases, see Galbraith and Karlin 2016. For a more general approach, see Jenkins 2006.

3. This is also part of a trend in online news consumption in general. See Dentsu. co.jp 2013, which includes summary sites not specifically tied to 2channel, such as *Naver Matome*, but also well-known 2channel sites. Part of the recent surge in popularity of these sites is also due to their mobile-phone interfaces and ease of use.

4. There are also Twitter accounts that summarize these summary sites, adding an additional layer of assisted reading to the equation. See, for example, @2ch_news, a *2chanmatome no matome* Twitter account that posts links to threads and stories from a variety of *matome* sites.

5. Lucas Hilderbrand has described the presence of links in a site's display as "introducing non-narrative seriality" that "replicates channel-surfing" by offering ease of access and indulging in distraction, a quality we can see in this type of presentation. Hilderbrand 2009, 227.

6. According to Akimoto (2014), the most popular *matome* sites generate over one hundred million views per month.

7. The sites were *Yaraon!, Hamster News Flash (hamusuta souhou), Hachima chihou, oretekigeemu souhou @ ha,* and *Nyuusoku VIP burogu*. Most of these sites did not survive the scrutiny that came with Hiroyuki's admonishment.

8. For some speculation about the future of *matome* sites in the wake of the announcement, see Tanaka 2011

9. An archived version of Hiroyuki's announcement can be found in IITmedia News 2014.

10. Parts of this period are explained and editorialized on in Anonymous Japan's website. See Anonymous Japan 2020.

11. See ibid. for a paraphrased version of Hiroyuki's explanation.

12. Users on reddit have complained about this. See a thread from /rjapan from June 15, 2015, for one example. Reddit.com 2015.

13. Other practices include altering the pitch of the soundtrack of a video—which is often done to avoid automated detection and claim some kind of difference from the original source—or adding content to the video image to claim differentiation from the original source. Some of these attempts at escaping copyright claims produce visually sophisticated modified version of commercial video content—essentially adding amateur overlays that simulate variety *telop* and related graphics interfaces—but their success at escaping copyright notices seems limited.

14. We might also compare this experience of time and impermanence in media to recent mobile phone applications that automatically delete photographs within a few moments after they have been shared, although this is not tied to copyright. See Kelly 2012 and Murray 2013.

15. For example, ratings for many weekly dramas during the highly desired "golden time" period (between 7:00 and 10:00 p.m.) failed to break 10 percent ratings, a far cry from the numbers that similar shows were obtaining only a few years earlier. Some critics have chalked this up to a drop in quality in the programming, but we should also recognize the shift in viewing habits due to media such as digital recording (DVR) and internet video sites that allow for alternative ways of watching. See Audience Rating TV 2011. A

*matome* site has also collected stories about some of the underperforming drams of 2011. Naver.jp 2011.

16. Nikkei BP Net 2009.

17. Andrew Kipnis (2012), for example, characterizes the internet in China as an "intensely national space" while arguing for a kind of communality organized around the nation-state through elements of regulation, censorship, nationalism, and language practices.

18. Indeed, the widespread (and perhaps disproportionate) interest in patterns of resistance in Chinese-language internet culture has often reproduced this ontology of the nation-state by investing all meaning-production on the horizon of the nation.

19. Lucas Hilderbrand gives a thorough account of VHS tape trading and the aesthetic properties of tape duplication in *Inherent Vice* (Hilderbrand 2009).

20. The possibility of Chinese-language video sites moving away from this more relaxed approach and toward copyright and embracing commercial partnerships with American and other foreign media is also something to consider. Clifford Coonan makes this observation in his story on the site's commercial licensing of American TV shows. See Coonan 2013.

21. Here I align myself with Lucas Hilderbrand's summation of a similar point, where he notes: "I agree with arguments against seeing new media as revolutionary; rather, new media reveal continuities, collaborations, and periods of coexistence as technologies change." Hilderbrand 2009, xiii. For elaboration on this type of stance toward television and new media, see Murphy 2011.

22. As Jason Karlin has noted in relation to advertising in television and online media, there is an intertwining of media forms that causes users to be "always conscious of television" in how they participate in internet media culture and the kind of content they engage with. Karlin 2012, 84.

23. For more on the integration of television staff into the laugh track of variety television, see Ota 2002, 51, 52.

24. The 2014 Hollywood horror film *Unfriended* uses a similar conceit, one that is more "integrated" into the experience of the viewer when watched on a laptop or computer, rather than a TV or movie theater screen.

25. Manovich 2006.

## 5. SCRIPTED LAUGHTER

1. Li 2017 uses the notion of "contact" to describe the relationship between *danmu* video and other forms of screen culture in China.

2. See Chin 2012 for a profile of one such figure, Adam Montoya, who went by "SeaNanners" while he was active on YouTube as a "let's play" video maker.

3. One of the main points of comparison is what is known as "gag communication" (*neta* communication). See Kitada 2005, 198–201; Hamano 2008a, 95; and Uno 2011, 150.

4. Videos in which the television screen or monitor is recorded by a video camera are sometimes referred to as "potato camera."

5. The ready availability of newer games and relative scarcity or expense of older systems also contributed to the popularity of emulation as an alternative way of producing these videos. Many contemporary consoles with internet capabilities also have built-in emulators that allow users to play older games. Some companies have started repackaging the equipment used for making these videos to target would-be video producers, advertising them as being made for console recording and using visuals associated with gaming to appeal to their new intended audience.

6. The differences in how the gaming industry responds to these sites are also worth noting as we consider their role in the promotional apparatus of the field. "Let's play" videos on YouTube have been challenged with some frequency by the gaming industry, such as Sega's attempt to remove videos of Shining Force III in November 2012 and Nintendo's claiming of ownership rights over a variety of videos in May 2013. For Niconico, many video makers avoid uploading video games while they are still considered new releases, to avoid the perception that they are competing with the industry. As such, *Boruzoi kikaku*—a well-established community of "let's play" video makers—was on the receiving end of considerable backlash from fans when they violated this unspoken rule in 2011 by making a video of a newly released game from the Donkey Kong series. For coverage of some of these events, see Geigner 2012 and Purchase 2012. For the Niconico incident, see BorzoiProject 2013.

7. Contemporary variety comedy in Japan has ditched the *manzai* duo for the most part, but the dual roles of *boke* and *tsukkomi* remain in many kinds of panels, interviews, and guest spots. There is an exaggerated legibility to the *boke/tsukkomi* constellation, and its circulation across so many performance forms has helped increase its grip on contemporary comedy in Japan.

8. Kitada's argument places this in a much larger history of the development of irony and cynicism in contemporary Japan, looking at events such as the 1972 Asama Lodge Incident and developments in consumer society during the period of the bubble economy to construct a trajectory for the emergence of "anti" culture and cynical laughter.

9. One significant difference is that these voice-overs are not always human voices; they are sometimes speech produced by voice-synthesizer software such as Vocaloid. The uploader "Razi-tama" has a series of *yukkuri* "let's play" videos in which the commentary is provided by a cast of characters who watch and play along together, all with voices made using voice-synthesizer software. One of these characters assumes the role of the player or narrator (called the "person inside"—*naka no hito*), and others appear as a supporting cast of helpers or comedic foils who are sometimes meant to also be in-game characters. As with Kitada's example of a variety TV show panel, this supporting cast will provides comedic commentary, making fun of the *naka no hito*'s mistakes or failures and referring to other parts of Niconico culture. The language of *naka no hito* is derived from fan culture commentary on voice actors and actresses.

10. The tendency toward *tsukkomi* on the Japanese internet is, according to Hamano Satoshi and Azuma Hiroki, based out of the culture of 2channel. They compare this to the antiestablishment nature of the site's user base and its tendency to cynically make fun of mass media and popular culture. Azuma, however, also notes a negative tendency in this kind of stance, comparing it to negative campaigning in politics and a violent tendency in some cultures of anonymity. He claims that the Japanese-language internet needs to move beyond (*sōtsugyō*) the *tsukkomi* tendency. Hamano and Azuma 2012, 179–81.

11. Ota 2003. Gerow 2010 compares Ota's formulation of *telop* to Azuma Hiroki's writing on database consumption.

12. The comments from the video for Mario 64 were from how the video appeared on February 20, 2012. For the video of Super Mario 3, the comment feed is from April 7, 2012.

13. The reason these videos are called "yukkuri" (which can mean "take it easy" or "take it slowly") is part of a chain of references, beginning with an old joke from 2channel. The catchphrase *yukkuri shiteitte ne* ("be takin' it easy!") was first associated with the image characters for Touhou Project, which were turned into ASCII art and posted widely across the forum. The phrase then appeared on Niconico in voice synthesizer videos of games using the Mugen software that replicated similar-looking characters. "Let's play" videos that use voice synthesizers have used the word *yukkuri* in their titles.

14. This resemblance is emphasized more in the comment feed by users who post (二) and (三) to approximate the face of the character as he dons the new suit and changes his face mask.

15. This is perhaps Hamano Satoshi's most well-received concept, introduced in his essay on the "generativity" of Niconico's tagging system. See Hamano 2008b, 313–54. The endless repetition of similar performances of laughter also suggests a kind of second-order performance or restatement of performance that is enacting citation as a kind of spontaneity.

16. This mode of initiation—and its reliance of familiar modes of participation—also asks us to couch this sense of play in the logic of ugliness or ugly ambivalence that substitutes predictable forms of meta-interaction for truly spontaneous instances of transformation.

17. This can be compared to the argument about transforming and self-annihilating archives in chapter 3.

18. Many Twitch streams essentially treat the game being shown onscreen as background noise for the conversation, which often tends to be about making fun of the player (if he or she is a well-known personality) or riffing on one another's jokes and messages. Using the chat to coordinate trolling-like behavior against the player can be thought of as an extension of this tendency.

19. This manner of recording does, however, produce a feeling of the depth of space the player is inhabiting that more professionally mixed recordings do not. The echo-like sound of the game coming from the television set or computer speakers can be heard as if coming from a short distance away, often with a muffled quality that places it as coming from a distinct spatial orientation other than that of the player's voice (which is closer to the microphone and picked up more clearly).

20. We should also keep in mind that some videos use an electronic voice synthesizer instead of the human voice of the player(s). This raises additional questions about a "non-body" and what kind of presence it might suggest. See Ishida 2008. Similarly, as Jacob Smith suggests in regard to recordings of vocal performance, even an individual voice can produce a presence of a non-body. Smith 2009, 45.

21. Smith characterizes vocal performance this way. Smith 2009, 86. It should be reiterated that some voice-over tracks are post-recorded or a mix of live and post-recorded narration.

22. One component in this performance and how it is interpreted by the Niconico audience is the politics of *kawaii* (cuteness). Yomota Inuhiko notes the relationship between *kawaii* and micro-aggressions toward girls, also noting how things like making mistakes or clumsiness (*shippai*) become a source of condescending sympathy (Yomota 2006). During the same video in which the players get excited about her success in defeating a boss, users in the comment feed begin transcribing what she says with emoticons used to represent her excitement (*nori nori*) and tone of voice. She thus becomes rendered as an icon in a way similar to the aesthetics of *kawaii* and manga and anime. This is also part of her performance, though, so we shouldn't understand this purely as a case of being passively victimized by abstract and structural qualities of gender. Rather, what is perhaps most salient is the way the gender-marked nature of that performance style (voice, language, etc.) is used and interpreted.

## POSTSCRIPT

1. Here I referr to Bakhtin's notion of the carnivalesque. Bakhtin 1982.

# Works Cited

Akimoto, Akky, 2014. "Who Holds the Deeds to the Gossip Bulletin Board 2channel?" *Japan Times*, March 20, 2014. https://www.japantimes.co.jp/life/2014/03/20/digital/who-holds-the-deeds-to-gossip-bulletin-board-2channel/#.XhO3XUdKjIV.
Alexa.com. 2016. "Top Sites in Japan." Accessed November 24, 2022. https://web.archive.org/web/20160201215436/https://www.alexa.com/topsites/countries/JP.
Allision, Anne. 2013. *Precarious Japan*. Durham: Duke University Press.
Altman, Rick. 1987. *The American Film Musical*. Bloomington: Indian University Press.
Anonymous Japan. 2020. "The 2channel Split Incident." Accessed January 11, 2020. https://www.anonymous-japan.org/fake2ch
Apter, Emily. 2005. *The Translation Zone: A New Comparative Literature*. Princeton: Princeton University Press.
Atkinson, David, and Helen Kelly-Holmes. 2011. "Codeswitching, Identity, and Ownership in Irish Radio Comedy." *Journal of Pragmatics* 43, no. 1: 251–60.
Audience Rating TV. 2011. [Statistics for 2011.] http://artv.info/ar1104.html.
Azuma Hiroki. 2014. *General Will 2.0: Rousseau, Freud, Google*. Translated by John Person. New York: Vertical.
———. 2011. *Ippan-ishi: Rousseau, Freud, Google* [*General Will 2.0: Rousseau, Freud, Google*]. Tokyo: Kodansha.
Bakhtin, Mikhail. 1982. *The Dialogic Imagination: Four Essays*. Translated by Caryl Emerson and Michael Holquist. Austin: University of Texas Press.
———. 1984. *Problems of Dostoevsky's Poetics*. Translated by Caryl Emerson. Minneapolis: University of Minnesota Press.
Ball, Christopher. 2004. "Repertoires of Registers: Dialect in Japanese Discourse." *Language and Communication* 24, no. 4: 391–435.
Bergson, Henri. 1990. *Matter and Memory*. Translated by N. M Paul and W. S. Palmer. Cambridge: MIT Press.
Berlant, Lauren. 2011. *Cruel Optimism*. Durham: Duke University Press.
Boellstorff, Tom. 2008. *Coming of Age in Second Life: An Anthropologist Explores the Virtually Human*. Princeton: Princeton University Press.
Bolton, Christopher, Istvan Csicsery-Ronay Jr., and Tatsumi Takayuki. 2007. *Robot Ghosts and Wired Dreams*. Minneapolis: University of Minnesota Press.
BorzoiProject. 2013. "Dodododododonkikongu nitsuite" [Concerning DoDoDoDoDonkey Kong]. FC2.com. Accessed January 16, 2023. http://borzoiproject.blog56.fc2.com/blog-entry-163.html.
Butler, Judith. 1990. *Gender Trouble*. New York: Routledge.
———. 1993. *Bodies that Matter*. New York: Routledge.
Chin, Anika. 2012. "'SeaNanners' and the Art of Videogame Commentary." *CNN Business*, May 7, 2012. Accessed November 24, 2022. https://www.cnn.com/2012/05/04/tech/gaming-gadgets/adam-montoya-seananners.
Chun, Wendy. 2005. "On Software, or the Persistence of Visual Knowledge." *Grey Room*, no. 18: 26–51.

———. 2008. "The Enduring Ephemeral, or the Future Is a Memory." *Critical Inquiry* 35 no. 1: 148–71.

Coleman, Gabriella. 2014. *Hacker, Hoaxer, Whistleblower, Spy: The Many Faces of Anonymous*. New York: Verso Books.

Coonan, Clifford. 2013. "Hollywood's New Goldmine: Youku Tudou." *Hollywood Reporter*, August 23, 2013. Accessed November 24, 2022. http://www.hollywoodreporter.com/news/chinas-youku-tudou-hollywoods-new-609112.

Crafton, Donald. 2012. *Shadow of a Mouse: Performance, Belief, and World-Making in Animation*. Berkeley: University of California Press.

Cubitt, Sean. 1991. *Time-shifted: On Video Culture*. New York: Routledge, 1991.

Cwiertka, Katarzyna, and Ewa Machotka. 2018. *Consuming Life in Post-Bubble Japan*. Amsterdam: Amsterdam University Press.

Dentsu.co.jp. 2013. "Dentsu PR Identifies 18.5% of Japanese as "Heavy Users" of News Aggregators." Accessed November 24, 2022. https://web.archive.org/web/20140306233317/http://www.dentsu-pr.com/news_releases/2012_07_31.html.

Doane, Mary Ann. 2002. *The Emergence of Cinematic Time: Modernity, Contingency, and the Archive*. Cambridge, MA: Harvard University Press.

Donnelly, K. J. 2014. *Occult Aesthetics: Synchronization in Sound Film*. Oxford: Oxford University Press.

Fedorenko, Olga. 2014. "South Korean Advertising as Popular Culture." In *The Korean Popular Culture Reader*, ed. Kyung Hyun Kim and Youngmin Choe, 341–62. Durham: Duke University Press.

Felisbret, Eric. 2009. *Graffiti New York*. New York: Henry Abrams.

Fukushima Ryōta. 2010. *Shinwa ga kangaeru* [Mythological Thinking]. Tokyo: Seidosha.

Galbraith, Patrick, and Jason Karlin. 2016. *Media Convergence in Japan*. [New Haven, CT]: Kinema Club.

Galloway Alexander. 2006. "Language Wants to Be Overlooked: On Software and Ideology." *Journal of Visual Culture* 5, no. 3: 315–31.

———. 2012. *The Interface Effect*. New York: Polity.

Geigner, Timothy. 2012. "Sega Goes Nuclear on YouTube Videos of Old Shining Force Game." *Techdirt*, December 7, 2012. Accessed November 24, 2022. https://www.techdirt.com/articles/20121206/17321021296/sega-goes-nuclear-youtube-videos-old-shining-force-game.shtml.

Gerow, Aaron. 2010. "Kind Participation: Postmodern Consumption and Capital with Japan's Telop TV." In *Television, Japan, and Globalization*, ed. Mitsuhiro Yoshimoto, Eva Tsai, and JungBong Choi, 117–50. Ann Arbor: University of Michigan Press.

Getnews. "*Hiroyuki-shi gat sui ni ugoita! 2channeru matome saito sonzoku no kigi ka*" [Mr. Hiroyuki Takes Action at Last! Is the Continuation of 2channel *Matome* Sites in Peril?]. Getnews.jp. http://getnews.jp/archives/274146.

Hall, Jeffrey J. 2021. *Japan's Nationalist Right in the Internet Age: Online Media and Grassroots Activism*. London: Routledge.

Hamano Satoshi. 2008a. *Aakitekutya no seitaikei—jyōhō kankyō ha ikani sekkei saretekita ka* [Ecosystems of Architecture: How Do Information Environments Come to Be Planned?]. Inuteitei Publishing.

———. 2008b. *Niconico Dōga no seiseiryoku* [The Generativity of Nico Nico Douga]. In *Tokushū: Generation*, ed. Azuma Hiroki and Kitada Akihiro, 313–354. Tokyo: Nihon Hōsō Shuppan Kyōkai.

Hamano Satoshi and Azuma Hiroki. 2012. "Aakitekucha *no seitaikei to sono go*" [After the Ecosystems of Architecture." In *Media wo kataru* [Talking about media], 142-214. Tokyo: Contextures.
Hamano Satoshi and Kobayashi Hiroto. 2010. "*Soosyaru nettwaaku no kanōsei—siea ha nani wo kaeru no ka*" [The Possibilities of Social Networks: What Will Sharing Change?], *Eureka* 43, no. 2: 51–52.
Hamano Satoshi and Sasaki Hiroshi. 2011. *Nihonteki social media no mirai* [The Future of Japanese Social Media]. Tokyo: Gijutsu Hyoron.
Heller, Monica. 2010. "The Commodification of Language," *Annual Review of Anthropology* 39, 101–14.
Herman, John, and Katie Notopoulos. 2013. "Weird Twitter: The Oral History." *BuzzFeed News*, April 5, 2013. Accessed November 25, 2022. https://www.buzzfeednews.com/article/jwherrman/weird-twitter-the-oral-history.
Hilderbrand, Lucas. 2009. *Inherent Vice*. Durham: Duke University Press.
Hill, Jane. 1993. "Hasta La Vista, Baby: Anglo Spanish in the American Southwest." *Critique of Anthropology* 13, no. 2: 145–76.
Hosoma Hiromichi. 2008. "Uta wo sodateta kanaria no tameni" [For a Canary Who Raised a Song] *Eureka* 40, no. 15: 30 – 52.
Huang, Betsy, Greta Niu, and David Roh. 2015. *Techno-Orientalism: Imagining Asia in Speculative Fiction*. New Brunswick: Rutgers University Press.
Inaba Hatate. 2011. "3.11 ga umidashi 'oshaberi' no rakuen [LINE] ni miru nihonteki intaanetto no yokubo" [The Pleasure Garden of 'Chatter' Born from 3.11: The Desire for Instant Gratification Visible in LINE], *PLANETS* 8: 52–59.
Inada Toshiaki. 2008. "Nihongo no boinyugo ni kan suru oboegaki" [Memo Concerning Vowel Coalescence in Japanese]," *Bungaku kenkyuu* [Studies in Literature], no. 105: 39–59.
Inoue, Miyako. 2006. *Vicarious Language: Gender and Linguistic Modernity in Japan*. Berkeley: University of California Press.
Irvine, Judith, and Gal, Susan (2000) "Language Ideology and Linguistic Differentiation," in *Regimes of Language: Ideologies, Politics, and Identities*, ed. Paul V. Kroskrity, Santa Fe: School for Advanced Research Press, 35 – 83.
Isaac, Mike. 2015. "4chan Message Board Sold to Founder of 2channel, a Japanese Web Culture Pioneer." *New York Times*, September 21, 2015.
Ishida Miki. 2008. "Naka no hito ni naru: bookaroido ga kanou ni sitamono" [Becoming the Person Inside: What Vocaloid Makes Possible], *Eureka* 40, no. 15: 88–94.
Iwabuchi, Koichi. 2002. *Recentering Globalization: Popular Culture and Japanese Transnationalism*. Durham: Duke University Press.
Jaffe, Alexandra. 2000. "Introduction: Non-standard Orthography and Non-standard Speech." *Journal of Sociolinguistics* 4, no. 4: 497–513.
———. 2011. "Sociolinguistic Diversity in Mainstream Media: Authenticity, Authority, and Processes of Mediation and Mediazation." *Journal of Language and Politics* 10, no. 4: 562–86.
Jaffe, Alexandra, and Shana Walton. 2000. "The Voices People Read: Orthography and the Representation of Non-standard Speech," *Journal of Sociolinguistics* 4, no. 4: 561–87.
Jenkins, Henry. 2006. *Convergence Culture: Where Old and New Media Collide*. New York: New York University Press.
Jorgensen, Kristine. 2011. "Time for a New Terminology? Diegetic and Non-diegetic Sounds in Computer Games Revisited." In *Game Sound Technology and Player Interaction*, ed. M. Grimshaw, 78–97. Hershey, PA: IGI Global.

Kanose Mitomo. 2010. "Garapagosu na Nihon no nettokai ni kaikoku wo sameru kurofune netto saabisu no rekishi" [The History of the Opening of Galapagos, Japan's Net-world, by the Approach of the Black Ships of Net Service," *Eureka* 43, no. 2: 68 – 80.

Karlin, Jason. 2012. "Through a Looking Glass Darkly: Television Advertising, Idols, and the Making of Fan Audience." In *Idols and Celebrity in Japanese Media Culture*, 72–93. New York: Palgrave.

Kelly, Heather. 2012. "Facebook Releases Poke App for Self-Destructing Messages." CNN, December 22, 2012. Accessed November 25, 2022. http://www.cnn.com/2012/12/21/tech/social-media/facebook-poke-app.

Kipnis, Andrew. 2012. "Constructing Commonality: Standardization and Modernization in Chinese Nation Building." *Journal of Asian Studies* 71, no. 3: 731–55.

Kitada Akihiro. 2005. *Warau nihon no nationalism* [The Sneering Nationalism of Japan]. Tokyo: NHK Books, 2005.

Kobayashi Hiroto. 2010. *Shiea* [Share]. Tokyo: NHK Books.

Kojima Hideo, dir. 2008. *Metal Gear Solid 4: Guns of the Patriots*. Konami. Playstation 3.

Li, Jinying. 2017. "The Interface Affect of a Contact Zone: *Danmaku* in Video-Streaming Platforms." *ASIASCAPE: Digital Asia* 4, 233–56.

Manovich, Lev. 2006. "After Effects, or, The Velvet Revolution." *Millennium Film Journal,* no. 45/46: 5–19.

Marks, Laura. 2002. *Touch: Sensuous History and Multisensory Media*. Minneapolis: University of Minnesota Press.

———. 2010. *Enfoldment and Infinite: An Islamic Genealogy of New Media Art*. Cambridge, MA: MIT Press.

———. 2011. "Calligraphic Animation: Documenting the Invisible," *Animation* 6, no. 3: 307–23.

Matsuda Kenjiro. 2006. "Netto syakai to syudango" [Net Society and Group-Language]. *Nihongogaku* [Japanese Language Studies] 25, no. 9: 25–35.

Mazzarella, William. 2010. "The Myth of the Multitude, or, Who's Afraid of the Crowd?" *Critical Inquiry* 36, no. 4: 697–727.

Miller, Ivor. 2012. *Aerosol Kingdom*. Oxford: University of Mississippi Press.

Miller, Laura. 2004. "Those Naughty Teenage Girls: Japanese *Kogals*, Slang, and Media Assessments." *Journal of Linguistic Anthropology* 14, no. 2: 225–47.

Mulvey, Laura. 1975. "Visual Pleasure in Narrative Cinema." *Screen* 16, no. 3: 6–18.

Murakami Naomichi and Ito Eisuke 2010. "Dōga tōkou saito de fuyo sareta dōga tagu no kaisōka" [Tag Hierarchy Analysis in Nico Nico Movie Service." *Zyōhōsyuri syakai kenkyū hōkoku* [Information Processing Society of Japan].

———. 2011. "Dōga sa-bisu ni okeru sityōsya komento no bunseki" [Analysis of the Comments of Video Hosting Service]. *Hi no koku zyouhō shinpoziumu* [Fire of National Information Symposium] March 18, 2011.

Murphy, Sheila. 2011. *How Television Invented New Media*. New Brunswick: Rutgers University Press.

Murray, Rheana. 2013. "Facebook Poke App Can't Beat Snapchat, but Questions Raised about Security." *New York Daily News*, January 2, 2013.

Natsuno Takeshi. 2011. "Nico nico dōga no koa ni aru mono" [In the Core of Nico Nico]. *Eureka* 43, no. 2: 81 – 89.

Naver.jp. 2011. "2011nen no teishichōritsu dorama to sono riyuu/hyōban" [The Lowest Rated Dramas of 2011 and Their Reasons/Criticisms]. Accessed November 30, 2019http://matome.naver.jp/odai/2132704362541473101.

Ngai, Sianne. 2007. *Ugly Feelings*. Cambridge, MA: Harvard University Press.
Nikkei BP Net. 2009. "Chugoku no douga saito ga nihon kara akusesu wo shadan" [Access to Chinese Video Sites Cut in Japan]. January 30, 2009. Accessed November 30, 2019. http://www.nikkeibp.co.jp/article/column/20090128/128044.
Nishimura, Yukiko. 2003. "Linguistic Innovations and Interactional Features in Casual Online Communications in Japanese." *Journal of Computer Mediated Communication* 9, no. 1. Accessed November 25, 2022. https://onlinelibrary.wiley.com/doi/full/10.1111/j.1083-6101.2003.tb00356.x
Nozawa, Shunsuke. 2012. "The Gross Face and Virtual Fame: Semiotic Mediation in Japan Virtual Communication." *First Monday* 17, no. 3. Accessed November 25, 2022. https://firstmonday.org/ojs/index.php/fm/article/view/3535/3168.
———. 2013. "Characterization," *Semiotic Review*, no. 3. Accessed November 25, 2022. https://www.semioticreview.com/ojs/index.php/sr/article/view/16.
Ota Shoichi. 2002. *Shakai wa warau: boke to tsukkomi no ningen kankei* [Society Laughs! The Human Relations of Manzai]. Tokyo: Seikyusha.
Patterson, Zabet. 2010. "POEMFIELDs and the Materiality off the Computational Screen." *Animation: An Interdisciplinary Journal* 5, no. 2: 243–62.
Phillips, Whitney. 2016. *This Is Why We Can't Have Nice Things: Mapping the Relationship between Trolling and Mainstream Culture*. Cambridge: MIT Press.
PHP Research Group. 2012. *Geemu jikyou no naka no hito* [Person Inside of Let's Play]. Tokyo: PHP Research.
Purchase, Robert. 2012. "YouTube *Shining Force 3* Content Suddenly Targeted for Copyright Infringement." *Eurogamer*. Accessed November 26, 2022. https://www.eurogamer.net/youtube-shining-force-3-content-suddenly-targeted-for-copyright-infringement.
Rasmussen, Terje. 2010. "Devices of Memory and Forgetting." In *The Archive in Motion: New Conceptions of the Archive in Contemporary Thought and New Media Practices*, ed. Eivind Røssak, 109–29. Oslo: Novus Press.
Reddit.com. 2015. "Japanese Matome-Sites Lifting Content from Reddit and Spreading Misinformation." *Reddit*. Accessed November 26, 2022. https://www.reddit.com/r/japan/comments/39wmqj/japanese_matomesites_lifting_comments_from_reddit.
Robertson, Wesley. 2022. "'Ojisan gokko shiyo!' [Let's pretend to be old men!]: Contested Graphic Ideologies in Japanese Online Language Play." *Japanese Studies* 42, no. 1: 23–42.
Rodowick, David. 2001. *Reading the Figural, or, A Philosophy after the New Media*. Durham: Duke University Press.
Roquet, Paul. 2016. *Ambient Media: Japanese Atmospheres of Self*. Minneapolis: University of Minnesota Press.
Saether, Susanne Østby. 2010. "Archival Art." In *The Archive in Motion: New Conceptions of the Archive in Contemporary Thought and New Media Practices*, ed. Eivind Røssak, 157–221. Oslo: Novus Press.
Sakai, Naoki. 1992. *Voices of the Past: The Status of Language in Eighteenth-Century Japanese Discourse*. Ithaca: Cornell University Press.
Sakamoto Mamoru. 1999. "Hanran suru jimaku bangumi no kouzai" [The Pluses and Minuses of Overflowing Subtitles on Television]. *GALAC*, June 1999. Accessed November 26, 2022. http://www.maroon.dti.ne.jp/mamos/tv/jimaku.html.
Sasaki Toshinao. 2011. *Kyureshion no jidai* [The Age of Curation]. Tokyo: Chikumashobo.

Scheible, Jeff. 2015. *Digital Shift: The Cultural Logic of Punctuation*. Minneapolis: University of Minnesota Press.
Silvio, Teri. 2010. "Animation: The New Performance?" *Journal of Linguistic Anthropology* 20, no. 2: 422–38.
Slater, David. 2010. "The Making of Japan's New Working Class: 'Freeters' and the Progression from Middle School to the Labor Market." *Asia Pacific Journal* 8, no. 1. Accessed November 26, 2022. https://apjjf.org/-David-H.-Slater/3279/article.html.
Smith, Jacob. 2009. *Vocal Tracks: Performance and Sound Media*. Berkeley: University of California Press.
Steinberg, Marc. 2017. "Converging Contents and Platforms: Niconico Video and Japan's Media Mix Ecology." In *Asian Video Cultures: In the Penumbra of the Global*, ed. Joshua Neves and Bhaskar Sarkar, 91–113. Durham: Duke University Press.
———. 2019. *The Platform Economy: How Japan Transformed the Consumer Internet*. Minneapolis: University of Minnesota Press.
Stewart, Jack. 2009. *Graffiti Kings: New York City Mass Transit Art of the 1970s*. New York: Henry Abrams.
Suzuki Kensuke. 2002. *Bōsō suru intaanetto* [Runaway Internet]. Tokyo: East Press.
———. 2006. *Kaanivaru ka suru shakai* [Carnival-becoming Society]. Tokyo: Kodansha.
Tanaka Yuria. 2011. *Hougen cosupure no jidai* [The Age of Dialect Costume Play]. Tokyo: Iwanami.
Tanner, Grafton. 2016. *Babbling Corpse: Vaporwave and the Commodification of Ghosts*. New York: Zero Books.
Taussig, Michael. 1999. *Defacement: Public Secrecy and the Labor of the Negative*. Palo Alto: Stanford University Press.
Taylor, Diana. 2003. *The Archive and Repertoire: Performing Cultural Memory in the Americas*. Durham: Duke University Press.
Tomabechi Hideto. 2011. *Majo no tettsui—gendaiban* [Malleus Maleficarum: Modern Edition]. Tokyo: Forest Publishing.
Tomita Akihiro. 2008. "Doujin ongaku no naka ni miru [Hatsune Miku]" [The "Hatsune Miku" we see within music circles]. *Eureka* 40, no. 15: 24–29.
Tseliga, Teresa. 2007. "It's All Greeklish to Me!" In *The Multilingual Internet*, ed. Brenda Danet and Susan C. Herring, 116 – 141, Oxford: Oxford University Press.
Tsunda Daisuke. 2009. *Twitter shakai ron: arata riaru taimu webu no chouryuu* [On Twitter Society: New "Real Time" and the Tide of the Web]. Tokyo: Yosensha.
Uchiyama Hiroshi. 2010. "Netto no nihongo: 2channeru to niconico douga wo tyuushin ni" [An Analysis of Japanese Used in the Net World]. *Kagoshima University Repository*, March 2010, 219–36.
Uno Tsunehiro. 2011. "TV no owari to intaanetto wandaarando?" [The End of TV and Internet Wonderland?"]. *Natsu yasumi no owarini* [Planets Special], 148–57.
Yamaguchi, Tomomi. 2013. "Xenophobia in Action: Ultranationalism, Hate Speech, and the Internet in Japan." *Radical History Review*, no. 117: 98–118.
Yanagita Kunio. 2010. "The Evolution of Japanese Festivals: from Matsuri to Sairei," translated by Stephen Nussbaum. In *International Perspectives on Yanagita Kunio and Japanese Folklore Studies*, ed. J. Victor Koschmann, Keibo Oiwa, and Shinji Yamashita, 167–202. Ithaca: Cornell University Press.
Yasuda Koichi. 2012. *Netto to aikoku: zaitoku-kai no yami wo wotte* [Nationalism and the Internet: Pursuing the Darkness of Zaitoku-kai]. Tokyo: Kansha.
Yomota Inuhiko. 2006. *Kawaii-ron* [On Cuteness]. Tokyo: Chikuma Shobo.

Zheng Xiqing. 2016. "Borderless Fandom and Contemporary Popular Culture Scene in Chinese Cyberspace." PhD diss., Department of Comparative Literature, University of Washington.

———. 2017. "Cheers! Lonely Otakus: Bilibili, the Barrage Subtitle System and Fandom as Performance." *Pop Junctions*, June 22, 2017. Accessed January 7, 2020. http://henryjenkins.org/blog/2017/6/15/cheers-lonely-otakus-bilibili-the-barrage-subtitles-system-and-fandom-as-performance.

# Index

accumulation, 75–78, 81, 93, 94, 96, 99
AcFun, 10, 19, 20, 26, 27, 28, 99, 103, 106
agency, 24, 29–30, 32–33, 68, 75–76
aggregate representation, shift toward, 24–25
Airman (character), 47, 48*fig*
alienation, 40
Allision, Anne, 4, 41
Altman, Rick, 121
Amazon Prime, 90
ambivalence, 103, 104–105, 107, 112, 114–121, 128
animation
    agency and, 29–30
    cel, 141n11
    concept of, 24
    performance and, 56–59
anonymous communication/anonymity
    elitism and, 4
    *matsuri* (festival) and, 67, 69, 71
    online culture and, 5–9, 11–12, 17, 18–20
    political tendencies of, 79
    polyphonic commenting and, 30–31
    social and aesthetic practices and, 80
    writing and, 15–16
Anthrax, 61
anticipation, 69
anti-Korean discourse, 1–2, 3*fig*, 5
"anytime/anywhere festival" (*itsudemo matsuri*), 29
appropriation, 91
Arabic writing, animation of, 57–58
Arino Shinya, 113, 114
Asama Lodge Incident, 146n8
ASCII art, 47, 53, 79, 140n10, 146n13
asynchronicity, 4, 9–10, 11, 17–18, 23, 130–131
Atkinson, David, 62, 63
augmented reality (AR), 27
authorship
    decentering of, 63
    displacement of, 65
    graffiti and, 53
    individual, 8–9
    *matsuri* (festival) and, 70
autocomplete, 32–33

autocorrect software, 142n21
Azuma Hiroki, 31–32, 33, 146n10

Bakhtin, Mikhail, 30, 56, 126
Ball, Christopher, 46
*Banana Cram School*, 13, 13*fig*
barrage commenting (*danmu/danmaku*), 8, 10, 17, 20, 26–28, 34–35, 62, 80, 82, 94–100, 137
Beastie Boys, 61, 74
belonging, network of, 17
Bergson, Henri, 71, 77
Berlant, Lauren, 41
Bilibili, 10, 19, 20, 26, 27, 28, 91, 92, 93, 94, 99
"blind" videos, 106
*Blood Clan Temple*, 80, 81*fig*
Boellstorff, Tom, 9
*boinyugo*, 142n30
*boke* (clown or fool), 109, 110–111, 126–128
*Boruzoi kikaku*, 146n6
*Bōyomi-chan* ("monotonechan"), 125
Butler, Judith, 81–83

"Can't Beat Airman," 10, 11*fig*
Capsule, 61, 74
captions/captioning, 34–35
cel animation, 141n11
centrality, 19
characterization, concept of, 43
"Ch-Check It Out," 74
China, 39, 41, 92–93
Chun, Wendy Hui Kyong, 65, 67
code of intimacy, 43
code-switching, 62
Coleman, Gabriella, 143n5
collection and curation, 85–89
collective unconscious, 31–32
*Coming Soon!* 98
comment art, 17, 21, 43, 47–53, 48*fig*, 49*fig*, 50*fig*, 55*fig*, 58, 72, 117–118, 122, 130–131
comment artists (*shokunin*), 117
commodification/commodified expression, 42–43, 45, 47
"contentless" communication, 70–71
Coonan, Clifford, 146n20

157

## INDEX

copy pasted writing, 8, 9
copypasta ASCII art, 8
copypasta writing, 78, 79
copyright
　deletions due to, 84
　summary portals and, 88–89
　video-sharing sites and, 90, 91–92, 94
Cornbread, 52
cosplay, 57
counter spectacularity, 17
Crafton, Donald, 141n1
curation, 82–83, 85–89
cynical nationalism, 139n4

Daft Punk, 61, 74
Dailymotion, 12, 26, 84, 91
Dance Dance Revolution (DDR), 115–116, 127
*danmu/danmaku. see* barrage commenting (*danmu/danmaku*)
data collection, 32
Daughter of Wota, 49
Davies, Christie, 144n13
DDoS attacks, 88
Dead Space, 118–119, 119*fig*
defacement of images, 21, 51–52
deletion, automated, 84
demagoguery, 68
de-nativization, 43
deviant script, 4, 24–25, 39–40, 44
dialect, alterity and, 46
dialect costume play, 44–46, 60, 62, 135
diegesis, 121–123
digital labor, 87, 94
disaster coverage, 144n13
disaster jokes, 78–79
Discord, 132
disengagement, self-presentation of, 5
distance, elitism and, 5
Doane, Mary Anne, 140n21
Donkey Kong, 146n6
Donnelly, K. J., 131
double vision of text and image, 53–56
Dr. Wily, 80
*Drummer Stands Out Too Much, The*, 61
Dustforce, 132
Dwango, 20

eBaum's World, 93
*edokokei*, 142n30
elitism, 4–5
emoticons, 58–59
ephemerality, 65, 67
erasure, 75–76

excitement (*nori*), 69, 76–77, 148n22
exhaustion, physical and mental, 4

Facebook, 20, 98, 107, 110, 135
face-cam, 113, 124
failure, 114, 126–128
fair use, 91
FC2, 26, 28, 86, 90, 91, 92, 99
Fedorenko, Olga, 140n15
fighting games, 80
figural aesthetics, 16
film studies, 121
5channel, 64–65, 89
foreign characters, use of, 37
forgetting, acts of, 77
4chan, 19, 88, 89, 143n5
fragmentation, 40
Fuji Television, 1–2, 3*fig*, 4–5, 6, 9, 21, 23, 113–114, 129, 136
Fukushima Ryōta, 36, 142n15
Futaba Channel, 8, 19
*futaba channel*, 89
Future Funk YouTube videos, 19

gag communication (*neta* communication), 146n3
gag-like (*neta-teki*) communication, 6, 68, 70–71
*Gaki no tsukai*, 114
Galloway, Alex, 15, 120–121
*Game Center CX*, 113–114
gameplay videos
　ambivalence and, 104–105
　asynchronicity and, 101–103
　types of, 103
　*see also* "let's play" videos
Gamergate, 19–20
Games for Windows Live, 123
Gekidan Hitori, 96
gender, language use and, 14–15
general will, 32
Gerow, Aaron, 146n11
globalization, 141n24
"'Go Die' is being used instead of greetings?! Actual state of the Judo world," 86–87
"God Knows," 72–74, 73*fig*
Google, 32–33, 38*fig*, 92, 143n7
Google bombing, 33
"Got the Time," 61
graffiti, 51, 52–53
Greek, romanization of, 62–63
group living (*shudan seikatsu*), 4

Habbo Hotel, 143n5
Hamano Satoshi, 21–22, 28–29, 31, 34, 63, 67–68, 69–70, 71, 76, 79–80, 107, 142n29, 146n10
"happening," 68–71, 87
hashtags, 144n12
Hatsune Miku, 27
Hayashi Osamu, 13
Heller, Monica, 15
Hilderbrand, Lucas, 145n5, 146n19, 146n21
Hill, Jane, 46, 61
*hiragana*, 36–37
Hirano Aya, 72–74, 73*fig*
Hitbox.tv, 107
*honkan*, 90
Hosoma Hiromichi, 48
hostages, return of, 68
hybridity, 99

"I Laughed at the Great Hanshin Earthquake!" 78–79
identity
  anonymity and, 4, 5
  disavowing, 4
  elitism and, 4–5
  loss of, 67
  stylization of, 4
ideographs, 36–37
"I'll Go to Tokyo," 74
image macros and memes, 8
image-oriented writing, 36
impermanence, 64–65, 66, 76–77, 85
in jokes, 80, 139–140n8
input method editor (IME), Japanese-language, 32–33, 37, 38*fig*, 57–58
Instagram, 20, 110
interface, 120–121
internet cafes, 140n14
intimacy, code of, 43
invisibility, dynamic of, 8
irony, concept of, 22
Ito Eisuke, 142n28
Iwabuchi Koichi, 141n24

Jaffe, Alexandra, 37, 141n3, 141n4
Japan, as context, 19–20
Japanese
  input method editor (IME) and, 32–33, 37, 38*fig*, 57–58
  typing and, 36–39
Jorgensen, Kristine, 122

Kadokawa, 20
Kansai dialect, 44
*kaodashi* (showing one's face) conventions, 110
Karlin, Jason, 146n22
*katakana*, 36–37
*kawaii* (cuteness), 148n22
Kelly-Holmes, Helen, 62, 63
*kigō-like (symbol-like) commenting*, 48
Kipnis, Andrew, 146n17
Kissasia, 91
Kitada Akihiro, 22, 109, 111, 114, 139n4, 139–140n8
*kyara* ("character") culture, 45

labor
  digital, 87, 94
  transformations of, 120–121
language
  approximating speech in written text, 43–44
  Japanese and, 32–33, 36–39, 38*fig*, 57–58
  nonstandard, 25
  in online platforms, 3–4
  text-to-speech applications, 125
  toyification of, 21, 43, 45, 46–47
language barrier, 92–93
language ideology theory, 46
"let's play" videos, 22, 75, 96, 103, 105–108, 110, 112–113, 115–120, 123–124, 127–128, 133
Li, Jinying, 141n6
linguistic play, 36–40
Livedoor, 86
"liveness" (*raibu-kan*), 12, 28–29, 35
livestreaming of gameplay, 103

Manovich, Lev, 99
*manzai* performance, 44, 109, 111, 126, 127
Mario 64, 116*fig*
Marks, Laura, 57–58, 140n10, 140n22, 143n7
*matome* (summary) sites, 84–89
*matsuri* (festival), 67–71, 87
Megaman 2, 80
Metal Gear Solid 4, 101–102, 104, 108, 110, 111, 115, 125, 127
Metropolitan Transit Authority of New York City, 53
micro-aggressions, 148n22
mimetic performance, 82
Mio Mio, 19, 92, 93, 94, 99
mishearing
  deliberate (*soramimi*), 21, 72–73, 80
  transcribed, 60–61
"Mishearing Awards," 61

## INDEX

"mistyping," 39, 41, 46–47, 58, 59, 60
Mixi, 135
Miyako Inoue, 35
*Mobile Suit Gundam*, 72–74, 73*fig*
monologic narration, 30
Mugen software, 146n13
Mulvey, Laura, 140n19
Murakami Naomichi, 142n28

*naka no hito* (person inside), 146n9
Nakai Masahiro, 98
Naoki Sakai, 56
nationalism, cynical, 139n4
Natsuno Takeshi, 141n9
*Naver Matome*, 145n3
"NEET," 80, 81*fig*
neoliberalism, 15
Netflix, 90
"netspeak," 25, 36
Ngai, Sianne, 105, 111, 139n5
Nico Nico Dōga, 27
Nico Shrine (*Nico jinja*), 129–131, 136
Niconico
  anonymity and, 6–7
  anonymous communication/
    anonymity on, 30–31
  asynchronicity and, 17–18
  cacophony of, 11*fig*, 12
  comment art and, 48
  comment text on, 27–28
  *danmaku* commenting and, 97–98
  defacement and, 52
  description of, 26–27
  double vision of text and image and, 54
  history of, 20
  linguistic play and, 36–40
  *matsuri* (festival) and, 71–72
  mishearing and, 61, 72–74, 73*fig*
  "mistyping" and, 62
  old messages and, 64
  overview of chapter on, 22
  personal pronoun usage and, 14–15
  presentation of time and, 29–30
  pseudo-synchronicity and, 9–10, 77
  repetition and, 81
  toyification of language and, 46–47
  translation and, 94
  typography and, 36–37
  United States of Odaiba event and, 1–2, 129–131
  user demographics and, 31
  video games and, 101–102, 103–104, 106, 109–112, 115–120, 121, 122

"Niconico Medley," 54, 55*fig*
Nihon Television, 109
Nintendo, 146n6
Nishimura Hiroyuki, 20, 88, 89
Niwango, 27
nonstandard language use, 25
normativity hangover, 41
Not Yet, 96
N.T. Technologies, 88
nth order derivative collaborations, 119

Odaiba event, 2, 3*fig*, 4–5, 9, 21, 23, 129–131, 136
*omae/omaera*, 14–15, 16, 135
online communities, studies of, 3–4
online festival (*matsuri*) culture, 22
*ore*, 14–15, 16, 135
orthography, standard versus nonstandard, 37–38, 41, 47
"Osaka," 118–119
Ota Shoichi, 111, 112, 114
overlooked, concept of being, 15–18

Painful News (*Itai nyuusu*), 86–87
parodic language, 61–62
Patterson, Zabet, 53–54, 56, 59
PC bangs, 140n14
performance
  animation and, 56–59
  mimetic, 82
  repertoire and, 66–67, 80
  repetition and, 81–82
personal pronoun usage, 14–15, 135
Pettit, Paul, 53
Phillips, Whitney, 33, 78–79, 143n5
phonetic transliteration, 62–63
piracy, 91
platforms, 140–141n23
PlayStation, 80, 106
plesiochronicity, 131–132, 136
POEMFIELDs videos, 53
Pokemon, 133
political agency, 4
polyphonic (term), 30
polyphonic commenting/narration, 30–31, 56
potato cameras, 146n4
P-P, 115–117, 117*fig*–118, 119, 122, 127
present
  problem of, 75–77
  sense of, 82
programming language, 15–16
pseudo-anonymity, 7, 9
pseudonyms/handles, 7

pseudo-synchronicity, 9–10, 21, 28, 71, 77, 108, 110
punishment games (*batsu geemu*), 114

raids, virtual, 143–144n5
Rasmussen, Terje, 77
ratings, 145–146n15
reaction artists (*riakushion geinin*), 128
recentering, 141n24
re-creation, 66, 82
reddit, 7, 88
rehearsal, aesthetics of, 77–83
repertoire, 66–67, 75, 80
repetition, 64, 66, 72–75, 80–82
right-wing political activism, studies of, 3
Rockman 2, 80
Rodowick, David, 143n3
roman letters, 36–37
Roquet, Paul, 139n6
Rousseau, Jean-Jacques, 31–32
runaway text production, 22

Sakai, Naoki, 126, 142n16
Sasaki Toshinao, 82
Scheible, Jeff, 142n21, 144n12
Sega, 146n6
selective synchronicity, 10, 29, 77, 142n29
self-deprecating humor, 80
self-documentation, 79
selfhood, unmarked, 8
self-presentation, 4, 14, 16, 19
September 11 attacks, 68, 78
"shared watching," 108–113
Shining Force III, 146n6
Shunsuke Nozawa, 17
Silvio, Teri, 57, 58–59, 143n6
Skype, 97, 98–99
Smith, Jacob, 126, 148n20, 148n21
social media
  anonymity and, 7
  fatigue and, 135
  inclusion of in shows, 98
  *kaodashi* (showing one's face) conventions and, 110
  simulation of, 100
  summary portals and, 84–89
  *see also individual platforms*
social reclusiveness, 4
software interfaces, 15–16
Something Awful, 19, 143n5
*soramimi*, 60–63
South Korean media, anti-Korean discourse and, 1–2, 5

space of friendship (*nakama no kuukan*), 111
*Space Sheriff Gavan*, 118
spectacle, 8, 15, 16–17, 79
speech, approximating in written text, 43–44.
  *see also* language
spontaneity, 68
Stardust Promotion, 139n2
"Starry Sky," 74
*Starrysky IKZOLOGIC Remix*, 61, 74
Steinberg, Marc, 139n1, 140–141n23
stereotypes, 46
Stream, 123
streaming, shift to, 90–95
Street Fighter II, 134
"Struck even two times . . .", 72–74, 73*fig*
suicide, rise in, 4
summary portals, 84–89
Super Mario 64, 116
Super Mario Brothers 3, 116, 117, 117*fig*, 118*fig*, 119, 122, 127
Super Mario Brothers franchise, 115
"Support Song for Victims of the Disaster," 75
Suzuki Kensuke, 22, 67–69, 71, 78, 144n7
"Sweet Magic," 49, 49*fig*, 72

tagging system, 34
Takaoka Sousuke, 1, 6, 9
Tamori (Morita Kazuyoshi), 60
*Tamori Club*, 60
Tanaka Yukari, 43, 44–46, 60
Taussig, Michael, 51–52
Taylor, Diana, 66, 75–76, 80, 143n2
"Technologic," 74
*telop* (television opaque projector) systems, 13, 13*fig*, 96, 97, 104, 112, 114
Tetris, 134
text-based communication, 9, 43, 45
text-laden video, 12–13
text-to-speech applications, 125
"thick" present, 71, 77
time
  cultures of, 67–72
  mediated experiences of, 66
  problem of present and, 75–77
  representation of, 64
  summary portals and, 87, 89
"time-shifted" media, 18
timing, disconnection and, 131–134, 136
Tokai Television, 13, 13*fig*
Toudu, 92
Touhou Project, 10, 146n13
toyification of language, 21, 43, 45, 46–47
transcribed mishearing, 60–61

transitional space, 57
translation, 94
transnational video networks, 91–95
troll culture/trolling (*arashi*), 69, 79
Tseliga, Theodora, 62, 63
*tsukkomi* (chastising figure), 109, 110–111, 116, 126–128
Tsunda Daisuke, 142n29
*TV That Will Make You Laugh*, 109, 127
Twitch Danmaku, 123
Twitch Plays Pokemon, 133–134
Twitch.tv, 22, 23, 103, 107, 110, 112, 123, 132–133, 136
Twitter, 1, 2, 6, 7, 9, 10, 29, 77, 86, 98, 144n12
2channel
  anonymity and, 6–7
  closing of, 64–65
  gallows humor on, 78–79
  *matsuri* (festival) and, 68–70
  Niconico and, 12, 20
  personal pronoun usage and, 14–15
  as point of reference, 26
  representation of time and, 64
  runaway text production and, 22
  static text and, 25
  summary portals and, 85–89
  time and, 66
  *tsukkomi* (chastising figure) and, 146n10
  United States of Odaiba event and, 1–2
2ch.sc, 88

UChat, 125
Uchiyama Hiroshi, 142n28
"ugly feelings," 105
*Unfriended*, 146n24
"Uninstall," 49, 50*fig*, 54, 55*fig*
United States of Odaiba (*Odaiba gashukoku*), 2, 3*fig*, 4–5, 9, 21, 23, 129–131, 136
unmarked selfhood, 8
UStream, 2, 3*fig*, 9, 107, 130

Vanderbeek, Stan, 53
Vaporwave, 141n26
variety television, 10, 13, 13*fig*, 22, 44, 60, 68, 103–104, 109, 111–112, 113–114, 128
video, online, 89–90
Vimeo, 12
Vocaloid, 27, 49, 119, 125, 146n9
voice, quality of, 123–126
voice synthesizers, 125–126
voice-over narration, 123–124, 125
VTubers (Virtual YouTubers), 19–20, 124

Walton, Shan, 141n4
Warcraft 3, 121
watermarks, 93
Watkins, Jim, 20
*We Are the Laugh Tribe*, 114
Weird Twitter, 140n9
well-wishers, 74–75
withdrawal, patterns of, 4
written text, speech and, 43–44

Xbox One, 106
xenophobia, 3
Xiqing Zheng, 10

Yanagita Kunio, 67
Yasuda Koichi, 139n3
Yauch, Adam, 74
Yoiko, 113
Yomota Inuhiko, 148n22
*Yonpara: Future Battle*, 96–100, 97*fig*
Yoshi Ikuzo, 61, 74
Youku, 26, 91, 92, 93–94
YouTube, 12, 22, 26, 84, 90, 91–93, 103, 106–108, 110, 112–113, 123, 141n12
Yukiko Nishimura, 31
*yukkuri* subgenre, 118, 125, 146n9

Milton Keynes UK
Ingram Content Group UK Ltd.
UKHW011813150923
428767UK00007B/247